MW01595128

Conflict to Cooperation:
A System for Mediating Differences

By Garry McDaniel, Ed. D.

in collaboration with
Barry Silverberg
Managing Editor, First World Library's
Nonprofit Leadership, Management and Organizational Development Series

Conflict to Cooperation: A System for Mediating Differences

Garry McDaniel, Ed. D.

© Garry McDaniel, Ed. D. 2002
F&F Publishing
1st World Library
8015 Shoal Creek Blvd., Ste. 100
Austin, TX 78757

First Edition

Senior Editor
Barry Silverberg

Cover Design and Production
Amelia Nottingham-Martin

Library of Congress Card Catalog Number:
ISBN: 0-9718562-3-0

Acknowledgments

This book would not have been possible without the support and insight of many wonderful people.

Diane Corley, J.D., spent invaluable time editing the manuscript and suggesting improvements.

Rexford Draman Ph. D., helped to refine the model presented in this book.

Barry Silverberg was the impetus for turning a valuable workshop into a book that can be shared widely.

Finally, Kathy Dominici and Stephen Littlejohn, Ph. D., contributed to the developing of a simple, practical and easily implemented process by which family members, communities, Board members, work teams and management can address and resolve conflicts.

Dedication

To
**Colonel Henry B.
and Irene
McDaniel**

Conflicting Thoughts

We believe that individuals and organizations can effectively deal with conflict. We believe that individuals, teams, coworkers and organizations are made stronger when conflict is transformed into collaboration. This requires a commitment to the dignity and worth of each individual and a desire to transcend the situation so that a cooperative resolution can be achieved.

Unproductive conflict remains a major impediment to significant organizational improvement and a barrier to positive relationships between people. But that need no longer be the case!

This guide, based on more than 20 years of collective work experience in industry and the nonprofit arena, provides executives, managers and employees with the knowledge skills and tools to turn conflict into cooperation. The principles and processes outlined herein apply equally within organizations, family, friendships and work environments.

Conflict need not be a prescription for poor performance and fractured interpersonal relationships.

Use this guidebook to try new approaches and reaffirm ones you may already be using.. While conflict may occur in all spheres of our lives, it need not be the unproductive and disruptive force it is for so many, Conflict can be transformed into cooperation!

Table of Contets

Unproductive conflict eats away at organizational quality, productivity and interpersonal relationships.

If you are working in today's adrenaline-fueled business environment, chances are pretty good that you have attended a class, workshop or seminar on the topic of conflict management. These are presented as part of training programs on communication, team development, interpersonal relationships, coaching, facilitation, and management skills. Bookstores and libraries are filled with conflict management literature. Colleges and universities offer graduate and undergraduate courses in it. And highly respected and competent institutes certify individuals as experts in conflict management.

Given all of these learning opportunities, you would think our lives would be conflict-free! **Yet unproductive conflict remains pervasive.** This is the case even when participants have attended conflict management workshops, read the literature, or are "certified" conflict resolution experts.

The title of this book, *Conflict to Cooperation: A System for Mediating Differeences,* reflects our belief, and experience, that the process outlined in these pages, when applied, can transform conflict into cooperation. All parties can achieve far greater satisfaction and effectiveness as a result.

Forward

*Cooperation
is the act
of working together
willingly to achieve
a common purpose*

We all experience conflict. It is a natural part of life. Similarly, .we have to cooperate to achieve individual and group success. Cooperation is the act of working together willingly to achieve a common purpose.

People are going to disagree. We are not always going to have the same approaches, goals or outcomes. We also know, from experience, that people have concerns and goals and take actions that if fully understood, can be jointly pursued to a successful resolution for everyone.

The conflict mediation system recommended in this book is based on the author's long experience in organizations as diverse as Fortune 500 companies, federal and state government, nonprofit organizations and community groups. The system can help organizations, management, employees and family members achieve greater alignment and synergy. It offers:

1.   **A set of principles** for continually improving the quality of work systems, roles, relationships and processes,

2.   **A practical, proven process** for creating a highly productive, fulfilling and motivating work or family environment, and

3.   **The skills to help** sustain the work environment created.

People have concerns, goals and actions that if fully understood, can be jointly pursued to a successful resolution for everyone.

**Conflict need not be a prescription for poor performance and frac-
tured interpersonal relationships.** The inability to deal constructively
and cooperatively through conflict is a prescription for poor performance
and fractured interpersonal relationships.

The process recommended in this book will help you move beyond conflict to success on the job, in your family and in all spheres of your life.

The book's format is intended to provide easy readability as well as plenty
of space for the reader to incorporate your own thoughts, perspectives, and
insights.

The author, and collaborating Managing Editor, welcome your comments
on the this volume, as well as suggestion of other volumes you would find
useful.

Send your thoughts to Barry Silverberg, Managing Editor, First World Library, 8015 Shoal Creek Boulevard,. Austin, TX 78757 or by e-mail to
barry@1stworldlibrary.com.

Garry McDaniel
Austin, Texas
September 29, 2002

How to use this guidebook

Using this guidebook as an individual

1. Read the book
2. Get an idea of the skills, knowledge and tools recommended
3. Learn the conflict mediation system
4. Set aside time each week t work through a specific problem or issue

Using this guidebook in a group:

1. Ask each member of the group to read the book to become familiar with the knowledge, skills and tools
2. Begin a dialogue regarding how well your group deals with conflict and where you might improve
3. Work through the implementation process
4. Periodically review your progress and improve

Using this guidebook as an organization:

1. Develop or review the vision and goals for your organization
2. Assess whether you can achieve those goals given your current level of conflict
3. Provide managers and employees with a copy of this book so they can become familiar with the knowledge, skills and tools
4. Convene a design team
5. Work though the imple mentation process
6   Communicate progress
7. Review progress & improve

Setting the Stage

Chapter 1

Conflict has a cost. The inability to work through conflict causes great stress among employees and management and suppliers that costs the organization time, money and ill-will with customers and suppliers.

Unproductive conflict costs organizations over $300 billion dollars a year in litigation expenses, according to Stewart Levine (1998). In addition, hundreds of millions of dollars have been spent on conflict management training, team building and interpersonal skills. BUT these annual expenditures are not being translated into effective, collaborative work.

Research indicates that the costs of conflict fall into several categories:

1. **Direct Costs** include litigation expenses for attorney fees, expert witnesses, trial and appeal.
2. **Productivity Costs** include the value of lost time, intellectual property, turnover, retraining and the **Opportunity Costs** of what those involved would otherwise have been producing.

Conflict costs
more than
$3 billion dollars
a year

What are the costs of conflict in YOUR organization?

_____

_____

_____

What are the costs of conflict in your work unit?

_____

_____

_____

What are the costs of conflict in your own personal life?

_____

_____

3.   **Continuity Costs** include the loss of existing relationships among ones network, customers, associates, vendors, suppliers, manufacturers, friends, etc.

4.   **Emotional Costs** include the turmoil and stress we feel when dealing with situations of conflict.[1]

In _The Magic of Conflict_ Thomas Crum shares the good news is that conflict does not have to be unproductive. He observes that conflict is a natural part of life.[2] Nature relies on conflict for change. It is the conflict within an oyster that creates a pearl. It is the conflict between water and land that creates beaches, vast canyons and mountain valleys.

Crum notes that conflict is as gift of energy in which neither side loses. It is the natural outgrowth of change, of improvement or movement away from the status quo.

Traditionally, conflict is defined as a situation in which "the ideas, interests or behavior of two or more individuals or groups clash."[3] There is nothing in the definition that suggests that conflict must be unproductive. Rather, it states conflict is when ideas, interests or behaviors of two or more individuals or groups are not in agreement - e.g., you may want to accomplish a task in one way, and I may want to accomplish that task in a different way. Our differences need not be unproductive.

Unfortunately, it is easy for conflict to become unproductive. Many working environments thrive upon constant change and competition, and our personal lives are often lived at a frantic pace. We try to be all things to all people by attempting to fit trips to the store, taking kids to band practice, rushing to get errands taken care of, and putting in eight to ten hours of work all in the same day. With all of these pressures it is no wonder that we have conflicts at home, on the way to work, within our work units, across divisions and companies.

Most organizations and families suffer the effects of unproductive conflict because they have no system for mediating conflict. What follows is designed to provide individuals, groups, teams and organizations with a framework for dealing with conflict effectively. It is based on the premise that those who comprise an interdependent group can mediate their conflicts if they share:

1. principles for guiding behavior and conduct,
2. a process for resolving conflict, and
3. the skills for effective communication.

We call this approach to conflict mediation a system because all three elements are interdependent; any major change in one causes a change in the others.

Interdependent groups can mediate their conflicts if they share:

1. principles for guiding behavior and conduct,

2. a process for resolving conflict, and

3. the skills for effective communication.

**How would you feel if you
were on the team?**

_____

_____

_____

_____

Organizations, work units and families are systems. They have an option of operating at a level in which they are highly creative, collaborative, cooperative and productive. They can deal constructively and honestly with conflicts and easily achieve and maintain this state.

On the other hand, we see many organizations and families that are abusive, dishonest, adversarial and defensive. They wonder why their productivity, interpersonal relationships and trust levels are poor. High levels of unproductive conflict are almost always characteristic of these entities.

To understand these three elements: Imagine that you are watching a professional baseball team and the team you favor is in the field. The opposing team's batter hits the ball to the shortstop, but instead of throwing the ball to the first baseman to get the runner out, the shortstop simply tosses the ball back to the pitcher and the runner is able to get on base safely.

After the game, the shortstop is interviewed on television and asked why he did not throw the ball to the first baseman to get the runner out.

"Well," the shortstop replies, "Yesterday the first baseman and I had an argument and I am not going to make him look good by throwing him the ball until he apologizes."

Does this incident reflect a clash between the ideas, interests or behavior of two or more individuals? Yes, The shortstop allowed a runner on base and could potentially cause the team to lose the game because he refused to cooperate with another player.

How would you react if you were the team owner? How do you think the other players would feel? What do you think other fans must be thinking? Wouldn't you be angry, disappointed, and incredulous? Wouldn't you feel justified in saying, "I don't care which team member you are angry at, your job on this team is to help us win the game!"

You may be thinking that this would never happen in 'real life.' After all, the players on a professional team would never be so petty in their behavior, would they?

Why do we have such high expectations of professional athletes?

First, professional athletes are **committed to principles that guide behavior and conduct** on the playing field.

Second, they have a strong and **well understood process** by which they play. This process includes the rules of the game, boundaries of the field, clear roles and responsibilities, sanctions for playing poorly (penalties, fines, loss of employment or endorsements, ostracism from other team members, bad press, etc.) and rewards for playing well (salary, bonuses, fan adoration, endorsements and so on).

Finally, they have developed and **continually practice their skills** and receive constant coaching to play the game.

Keep this in mind as you read the next scenario.

Wendy Brown is the owner of First Amalgamated Widgets, one of the 'up and coming' companies in the widget industry. If growth continues as it has in the past, the company is sure to receive a significant influx of funds from investors. One day, Wendy receives a phone call from one of their biggest customers stating that they are not happy with the quality of the widgets they have been receiving. The customer advises Wendy that they are returning the last order received and will refuse to accept any further deliveries until the problem is resolved.

Anxious to get to the bottom of this problem, Wendy assures the customer that she will investigate the problem. She hurries down to the manufacturing floor to talk to the production supervisors. When she arrives, the evening shift change is taking place.

As Wendy waits for the shift change to be completed, she notices that members of the first shift are not making any effort to communicate the status of the equipment or explain where the various types of widgets are in the production process before they leave for the evening. Wendy knows that it is vital that the incoming shift understand which pieces of equipment are running properly, are having problems, or need to be taken down for maintenance. She also knows that it is important to understand at which step in the assembly process a widget is so that errors are avoided.

Wendy stops the outgoing shift supervisor and asks why his departing shift is not ensuring that the incoming shift members completely understand the equipment and production status.

"Oh," the supervisor replies, "A couple of weeks ago, I was trying to explain a potential production problem at our shift change meeting. The supervisor of the second shift didn't agree and made me look like I didn't know what I was talking about. After making me look bad in front of everyone, you can bet I'm not going bring that problem up again. Now that the production has gone downhill just like I said it would, we'll see how stupid she looks for a change!"

Wendy replies, "But certainly you realize that a poor pass-down process must mean that over the past few weeks the quality of the widgets we have been shipping must be below our customer's requirements don't you?"

"Of course," he says, *"And this will just prove that I was right and she was wrong!"*

How would you react if you were Wendy? Your best customer is sending back a full shipment of widgets and refusing to accept others because one employee refused to cooperate with another. Wouldn't you be angry & disappointed? Wouldn't you feel absolutely justified in saying, "I don't care which other employee you are angry at, you're paid to produce high quality widgets!"

How would you react if you were in Wendy's shoes?

_____

_____

_____

_____

_____

_____

The big question: How is this situation any different than that described with the baseball team? Aren't both of these individuals paid professionals? Aren't they supposed to be working together with the rest of the group? Isn't 'winning the game,' 'making the sale,' 'reducing scrap,' 'being first to market,' 'improving quality' or 'working as a team' what it is all about? The two situations are almost identical.

The difference is that on the playing field, unproductive conflict is apparent to everyone. The players, fans and coaches understand the skills, process of the game and operating framework required so well that deviations from the standard of excellence are clear.

In the workplace, we often ignore or deal with unproductive conflict until it hits crisis proportions.

Collaborative Work Groups

Organizations rely upon employees to work interdependently because it is simply good business. The design, development, manufacturing and sales of products and delivery of services can be significantly enhanced by highly functioning collaborative work groups. Studies conducted by the Center for The Study of Work Teams document that groups which work collaboratively are more effective in assisting organizations to:

1. Improve service delivery
2. Meet or exceed customer needs
3. Introduce improvements and/or innovations
4. Integrate and streamline organizational structures, systems and processes
5. Design, develop and produce products
6. Enhance employee morale and retention
7. Speed new employee orientation and training
8. Reduce costs and inventory while increasing product or service quality[4]

Organizations rely on employees to work interdependently because it is simply good business!

Where group collaboration is lacking or inefficient, service delivery falters, customer needs are not fulfilled, improvements or innovations lag, and maintaining the status quo becomes the norm as product cycle times suffer. Instead of increased profits and job security, profits fall and people worry about the long-term safety of their jobs.

In these and similar studies organizations and group members also identified sources that not only saps the efficiency and effectiveness of organizational work environments, but causes great stress among employees and management.

What are some of the sources of conflict in your organization?

_____

_____

_____

_____

_____

Sources of conflict include situations in which management and employees:

1. Consistently arrive to work late, take breaks early, and come back from breaks late
2. Avoid helping orient or train other employees
3. Show little interest in learning new skills or taking on new responsibilities
4. Intentionally belittle, put-down, or tease other employees
5. Fail to communicate needs or expectations and then get angry at those who do not understand
6. Punch the clock' and go home, never staying late in a crisis

7.   Refuse to share tools, information or supplies with others that are vital to the work being accomplished
8.   Form cliques that side against other employees or work units

If unproductive conflict has such negative consequences, why do we expect so much from professional athletes, and so little from managers and employees in organizations?

Managers and employees are also paid and trained to apply work-related and interpersonal skills, to work effectively within the organizational process and to be committed to the organization. Shouldn't managers and employees hold each other accountable to strong group principles? After all, managers and employees recognize that violating the rules of work or behavior with other team members results in decreased productivity and possibly punishment (suspension, loss of employment, ostracism from other team members, etc.) And, work groups usually receive training in team skills and behaviors so that they are able to maximize the positive outcomes expected of the group.

What may be missing is a system by which managers and employees see a direct link between helping the group to succeed and potential reward such as increased salary, bonuses, positive recognition from co-workers and so on.

Shouldn't managers and employees hold each other accountable to strong group principles?

Methods for dealing with conflict:

1.   Avoidance

2.   Accomodation

3.   Compromise

4.   Competition

5.   Collaboration

Organizations, work groups, families and Boards can and should be able to work to a higher standard than they do. By understanding how others respond to situations of conflict you will be in a better position to deal with conflict constructively.

The first method for dealing with conflict is avoidance. Avoidance occurs when one shuns conflict non-verbally or emotionally. By minimizing a problem, making light of a situation, changing the subject, or joking about a conflict, people avoid the area in question. When an organization, management or employees avoid conflict, they run the risk that the conflict will escalate and the divisions between groups or individuals will widen.

A second method of responding to conflict is accommodation, or 'giving in.' Accommodation may occur at any level within an organization. For example, organizations may make unilateral policy changes affecting the workforce and simply expect employees to 'fall in line.' If one group member is a single parent and must arrive at work late due to a daycare schedule, the group and management may simply accept this fact and work around the issue.

'You give half and I give half' is the description we often hear for the third method which is compromise. Compromise often occurs after an impasse or stalemate when two groups feel they can't make any additional headway in their negotiations. The risk with compromise is that the groups may be giving up something that they really need or want. This leads to dissatisfaction and may ultimately undermine the solution that is agreed upon.

In the fourth or competitive approach, the person with the most power in terms of time, money, resources, position or communication style negotiates from a 'I win, you lose' point of view. This method often provokes defensiveness and leads the other party to dig in their heels thereby bringing the negotiations to a halt. Those group members who continually wind up on the losing end of the negotiation will generally respond by passive aggression, withholding information, effort, or otherwise 'getting back' at the individual who 'won.'

The final approach people use when dealing with situations involving conflict is to collaborate. Collaborative method is preferable for organizations and groups which need a method for managing conflict that respects the needs of others and enables them to freely assert their own needs and wants. Collaborative decision-making assumes that the parties involved want to achieve a mutually satisfactory, or 'win-win' solution.

Collaborative decision-making assumes that the parties involved want to achieve a mutually satisfactory, or 'win-win' solution.

Collaborative decision-making does not mean that all group members have to be great friends or that they agree with each other. Collaborative decision-making assumes that the parties can create enough options, choices or solutions for each side to find satisfactory agreement.

The Value of Group Collaboration

Groups that work collaboratively have clear advantages over those that cannot resolve their conflict. These advantages include:

1.   increased pride and ownership of work,

2.   enhanced morale,

3.   higher productivity and efficiency,

4.   greater staffing flexibility,

5.   sharing of resources, and

6.   increased challenge on the job.

In groups where conflict has become a continual pattern, employees and work units frequently build barriers between themselves or look to management to step in and 'solve' their conflicts. Neither approach works well in practice.

In groups where conflict has become a continual pattern, employees and work units frequently build barriers between themselves or look to management to step in and 'solve' their conflicts

Cliques, backstabbing and barriers simply create discord and wastes productive time and energy. Looking to management to 'solve' a conflict absolves those in conflict from responsibility and often does not solve the problem anyway. However, if managers empower employees to resolve their own conflicts, the manager is freed up to focus on higher level work in continuous improvement, strategic planning, and in mentoring and coaching of team members.

When asked, groups suffering from unproductive conflict give several reasons:

First, they suggest that despite the fact that they have received conflict management training, they have little incentive to use the skills. Not only are their skills lacking, they also note that their management does not know how to coach group members to mediate conflict.

Second, group members observe that they do not have an adequate process for resolving disagreements, negotiating increased responsibility and accountability for their work and holding each other to a high standard of team effectiveness.

Finally, employees and management report that they lack guidelines that allow them to hold each other accountable for behaviors and actions.

If managers empower
employees to resolve
their own conflicts,
the manager is freed up
to focus
on higher level work

Without any incentive to use their skills and the absence of a coherent process to follow, employees have little commitment to resolve conflicts; it is easier just to let them fester or pass them on to management.

Conflict to Cooperation

The Conflict Mediation System presented in these pages provides organizations and individuals with a method for resolving the conflicts that act as barriers to productivity, efficiency and which cause stress, frustration and wasted effort in life The system helps you to recognize and resolve conflicts productively at the lowest possible level. The importance of this latter point cannot be overlooked.

If not addressed in a productive fashion, organizations and individuals avoid dealing with the conflict which leads to bad feelings, lowered productivity and poor morale. Employees may also look to management 'to solve' the conflict for them. This is not productive as it absolves the employees of responsibility, wastes time and productivity. When management provides a solution, it is management's solution, not those involved. Finally, resolving conflicts that others could mediate themselves keeps management from focusing on higher level work.

Without any incentive
to use their skills
and in the absence
of a coherent process
to follow, employees
have little commitment
to resolve conflicts;
it is easier to let them
fester or pass them on
to management.

The conflict mediation system (Figure 1) is comprised of three elements that fit together like the pieces of a puzzle:

1. **Principles** for guiding behavior and conduct
2. A **process** for mediation conflict at the source whenever possible
3. The **skills** to communicate effectively with others in situations where conflict is present

Figure 1
Conflict Mediation System

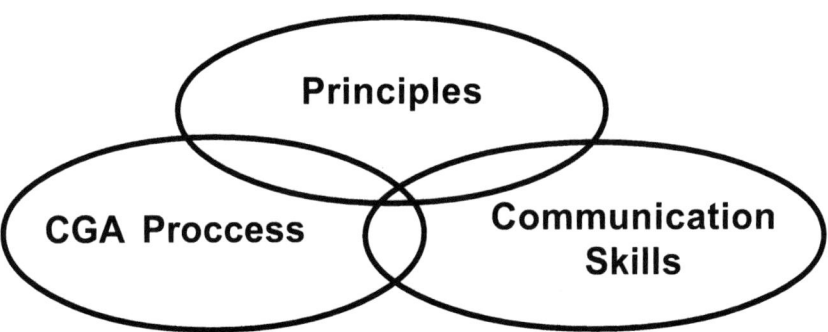

These elements will be explained in greater detail in the chapters ahead.

This system can be helpful for addressing conflict situations of and for supporting other organizational growth and change efforts. For example, the process can assist employees and management establish a framework for identifying tasks that for which the employees can and should take ownership for transferring the responsibility, accountability and rewards for exceptional results. The system can also provide an avenue for allowing the organization and employees to resolve past or existing inequities.

Most organizations and groups must begin the conflict mediation system with some history. It may be a well-deserved history of mistrust, abuse and confrontation between management and employees. Team members may have deep interpersonal rivalries and grievances against each other. Work units or divisions may have deeply entrenched silos with powerful ego's that must be dealt with. Each of these must be carefully and humanely dealt with and resolved for the organization and its employees to move forward.

"The significant problems we face today cannot be solved at the same level of thinking we were at when we created them"

Albert Einstein

Albert Einstein observed, "The significant problems we face today cannot be solved at the same level of thinking we were at when we created them" (cited in *Seven Habits of Highly Effective People*, Covey, 1989, p. 42)

Continuing with the same systems, processes, expectations and behaviors you have in place is not going to move the organization or collaborative work groups to a higher level of operations.

It is critical to recognize that with a change of this magnitude, not everyone is going to want to play the game by the new rules. Some people are going to decide that the status quo is comfortable and that change is just a little too threatening. Metaphorically, they are going to announce by action or inaction that they are not going to 'play ball' with everyone else. When this happens - and it will happen - you must be ready to decide if they are going to continue playing on your team, or if they need to find some other place to play. If nothing happens, then nothing has changed.

In the next chapters, you will learn the process and skills that make up the conflict mediation system.

In Chapter 2, you will learn how to work as an organization to identify the principles that define the path to become a truly high performing collaborative organization.

In Chapter 3, we describe the three-step process of conflict mediation.

In Chapter 4, we present the basic skills needed to assist managers and employees to confront and deal with conflict.

In Chapter 5, you will have the opportunity to practice the system and the skills you have learned.

**If nothing happens,
then nothing
has changed.**

In Chapter 6, you will learn the role of the manager or group leader in making this transition and how to determine when a third party mediator is needed.

In Chapter 7, we cover the broader applications of the system to areas outside of the traditional workplace.

---

[1] Getting to Resolution. (1998) Steward Levine. Berrett-Koehler, San Francisco.
[2] The Magic of Conflict (1987). Thomas Crum
[3] Controlling the Costs of Conflict: How to Design a System for Your Organization. Karl A. Slaikeu & Ralph H. Hasson. (1998). Jossey-Bass Publishers, San Francisco, California, p. 6.
[4] Linking Support Systems to Team Effectiveness, 1999, Christopher A. Hall and Michael M. Beyerlein.

Defining the Road to Success

Chapter 2

Y ou don't have to be the CEO of a Fortune 500 company to recognize that organizational survival in today's rapidly changing
business environment is difficult.

Survival and growth involves continually enhancing employee skills, and
staying abreast of new markets while maintaining increasingly high levels
of research, design and production. Change of this magnitude is almost
guaranteed to cause conflict.

To collaborate together effectively, organizations and individuals must
manage conflict in ways that are conducive to a synergistic and highly
productive work environment. Inevitably, workers are going to have disputes over roles, responsibilities, and resources. Nevertheless, they must
be able to work through these disputes quickly and effectively.

Disputes and mistrust between management and employees can easily
backfire and create oppressive, inefficient work environments that de-
grade the organization's effectiveness.

**Change
is almost guaranteed
to cause conflict**

In a world where every second and every cent counts, those organizations that can productively manage day-to-day conflicts will come out on top in the long-term.

In this chapter you will learn how an organization and individuals can define principles for developing a highly productive environment. The conflict mediation system is based upon principles for guiding behavior and conduct, a process for mediation conflict at the source and the skills for communicating effectively with others in situations where conflict is present.

For example, in any sport there are principles of how the game is played, the physical dimensions of the playing area, tools that one plays with and what the rules that constitute proper and improper play. These same principles provide structure, organization and purpose for both the players and the fans. The principles are not a constraint upon the game, rather they allow the players to be as free and creative as they can within the framework of that sport.

Similarly, the conflict mediation system recommended in this book is built upon principles from which people may operate on a day to day basis. These principles provide all group members with a clear idea

The conflict mediation
system recommended
in this book is built upon
principles from which
people may operate
on a day to day basis

of what 'success' looks like and define how the members will operate and support each other to achieve success.

Five principles provide the minimum framework (Figure 2) for a productive, motivating and empowering workplace.   The principles are-

1.   **Organizational values**

2.   **A safe environment**

3.   **Collaborative communication skills**

4.   **Power management**

5.   **Process leadership**

Principles
provide all group members
with a clear idea of what
'success' looks like
and define how
the members will operate
and support each other
to achieve success.

Figure 2
Conflict Mediation Principles

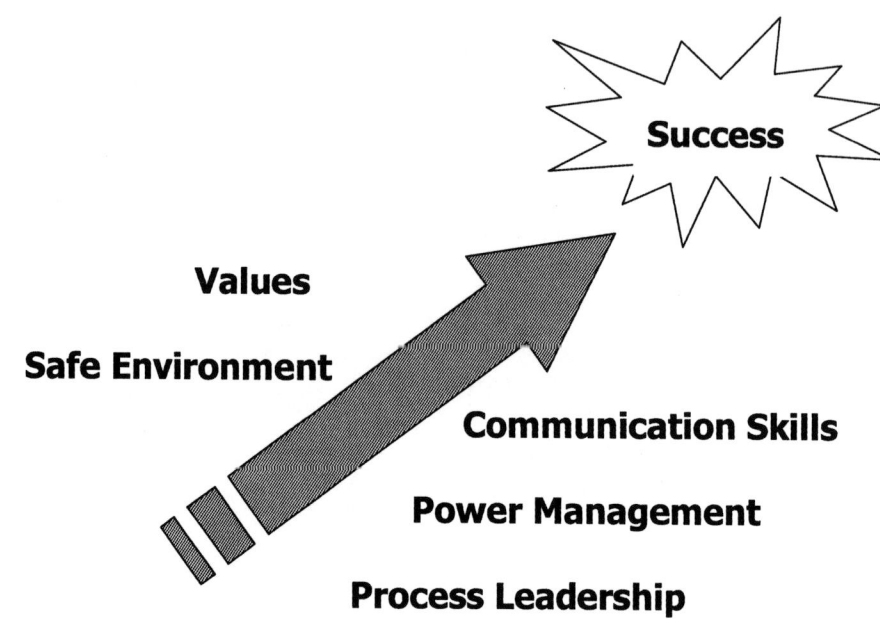

You may choose to name the five principles something different that has more meaning to your work environment. You may add another principle or two that are particularly important in your industry or culture. But, establish those principles in a clear and credible fashion.

Laying Out the Road

An easy way to visualize the principles is to think of them as the boundary or curb on your road to success. You start wherever you are right now and the road leads to whatever you define as 'success.' The principles help you set your direction and allow you and others to know when you are 'on track' or veering off course.

Success in your organization may be profitability, new products, better service, better quality, improved relationships, or any number of worthwhile outcomes. Success in your family may be personal growth, education, financial security or healthy lifestyles.

Each principle will be described briefly to help you understand how each supports the entire system. Recommendations for designing and developing these five principles within your organization, division or work group will be elaborated upon in Chapter 6.

Organizational Values

What does "agreeing to a set of shared values" really mean? Values inform us of what to do and what not to do, according to Kouzes & Posner, (1993)[5]. Values become the standards of our actions and behaviors, our attitudes towards others and how we treat other people.

When values are clear, credible, and enacted consistently by everyone within an organization, employees do not have to look to someone in authority for direction. Rather, employees are able to act in a responsible fashion that benefits themselves, and others over both the short and long-term.

Values provide a means for addressing conflicts and for making decisions. Sometimes, the needs of the group and organization may outweigh the needs of the individual. On other occasions, the organization and group may decide to support the individual.

A group member may value both paying appropriate attention to one's family and customer service. When faced with staying late to respond to a customer service request or leaving on time to make a family responsibility, the employee can foster a constructive discussion with coworkers by communicating their values.

When values are clear,
credible, and enacted
upon consistently
by everyone
within an organization,
employees do not need
to look to someone
in authority for direction.

Creating a Safe Environment

Effective organizations create a safe environment where members are skilled at communicating with each other about thoughts, ideas and conflicts. They create environments in which managers and employees feel recognized and appreciated for working well with others and enhancing group success.

Abraham Maslow identified five levels of human motivation in his 1943 theory of human motivation based on a hierarchy of needs. As presented in Figure 3, these are:

1.   **Physiological needs** which include basic human biological functions such as hunger, thirst, sleep and sex.
2.   **Safety and security needs**, or the requirement for a secure environment.
3,   **Love and social recognition**, or the need for belonging and connection to others.
4.   **Esteem needs** or the need to be regarded well in terms of achievement and recognition.
5.   **Self actualization**, which is when people feel they are doing what they were best suited for, fulfilling life goals and realizing their potential.

It is important to satisfy one level in the hierarchy before moving to the next level, according to Maslow. This directly relates to organizational, team and family dynamics.

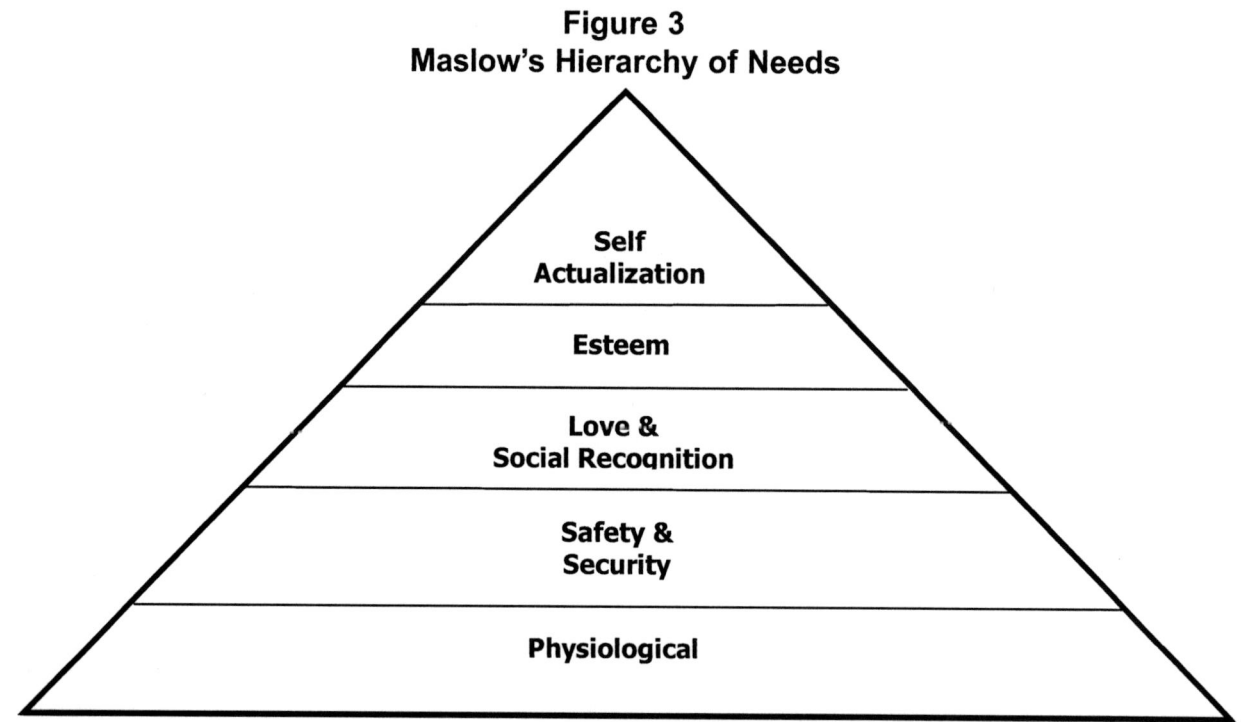

**Figure 3
Maslow's Hierarchy of Needs**

Many organizations fail to realize that productivity and effectiveness result from a highly self-actualized workforce. The same is true within teams and families.

We all want unbridled growth and prosperity. But if the work environment is one in which employees and management do not feel safe to voice their concerns and needs, then little actualization will occur.

If team or family members do not feel safe, they will not perform or behave to their capability.

Communication Skills

People need to be able to express their ideas, voice their concerns and share suggestions in the normal course of interactions. Communication is more than just speaking one's mind. It is also listening.

Few of us have had serious training in listening, though many of us have had courses in public speaking or presentation skills. Yet more than anything else it is our capacity to listen, and to truly "hear" the other person, that is the prerequisite to any conflict mediation system.

What type of work environment brings the best out in you?

_____

_____

_____

_____

_____

_____

The communications skills necessary to be effective with the conflict mediation system proposed in this book can be summarize in an acronym, "CLARC".

Confront or bring a problem or issue forward to be collaboratively examined

Listen or hear what the other person has really said

Acknowledge or ensure that you have heard what the other person has said

Respond or provide your perspective, checking for understanding or gathering additional information

Commit or agree to move to further discussion or action steps

Each of these skills will be described in greater detail in Chapter Four..

Confront

Listen

Acknowledge

Respond

Commit

Power Management

Power management recognizes that employees of all levels bring capabilities that can help drive the organization or group forward. Power management is the process through which team members and employees recognize, acknowledge and work with their differences. When a person dictates actions due to positional power, others may sit back and cease to contribute, become argumentative or avoid involvement altogether. Organizations should leverage these varying skills for the good of all concerned; rather than allow any one party 'to get one's own way.'

When one person dictates actions due to positional power, others may sit back and cease to contribute, become argumentative or avoid involvement altogether. Power management is the process through which team members recognize, acknowledge and work with their differences.

Process Leadership

The most effective groups identify someone to serve as a group process facilitator. This person ensures that the group is true to its principles, focused on the issues being discussed, and that all members participate.

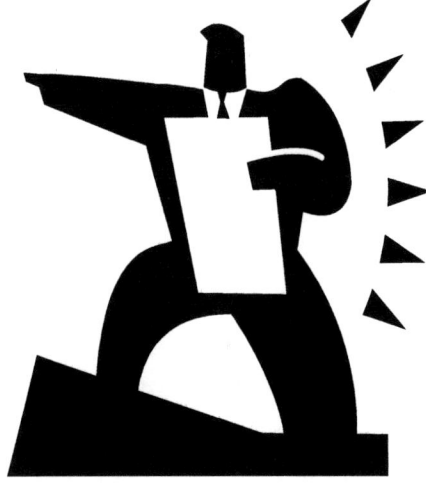

Group process leaders should be skilled at helping others to evaluate problems, arrive at decisions and develop action plans. Process facilitators use a variety of group methods such as brainstorming, force-field analysis, flow-charting, fish-bone and affinity diagrams and multi-voting.

Selecting a person as process facilitator does not imply any power to the person other than they are to focus on managing the conflict mediation process. The process facilitator clarifies communication, prevents miscommunication and assists the group in the application of appropriate problem-solving and decision-making methods.

Stepping Off The Road

Even the most committed, motivated, well-meaning individual **occasionally makes a mistake or takes an action that is in opposition to group values.** It is important to recognize that our reactions to others are most often unintentional and not always directed at anyone in particular- it's just that we happen to 'snap' at someone due to our stressed state of mind. A stressful morning getting the kids off to school, a lingering cold, traffic jam, spilled coffee on one's desk or any number of other minor irritants can cause us to behave or react to others in ways that we would agree are not productive.

Selecting a person
as process facilitator
does not imply
any power to the person

Defining the Road to Success

Team members can continue to build trust and maintain group integrity by defining principles for guiding behavior and conduct and developing the skills to address the transgression in a way that is supportive and understanding.

When a supportive coworker helps us become aware that we have violated a shared value, or communicated in a way that was hurtful, it is easier for us to move back to the path of behavior that we all agree is best for everyone.

When situations of conflict allow for an uncomfortable or unsafe environment, team members are more likely to respond with avoidance, accommodation or competitive methods.

Collaborative decision-making can result only if the organization and employees are committed to, and skilled in the use of a mediation system that encourages the search for understanding and growth. Such a system facilitates the positive discussion that allows everyone to maintain face, feel they are "heard" and valued.

This is a foundation to the conflict mediation system we now present.

---

[5]Credibility. (1993). J. Kouzes & B. Posner. 1993. Jossey-Bass Publishers, San Francisco.

Collaborative decision-making can result only if the organization and employees are committed to, and skilled in the use of a mediation system that encourages the search for understanding and growth

Notes

The Road to Success

Chapter 3

Most conflicts are recognizable when the individuals involved express a position. Positions are usually communicated in a statement such as, 'What I want, what I suggest.., or what I need...' As illustrated in Figure 4, such a position is really just the tip of the iceberg. The more

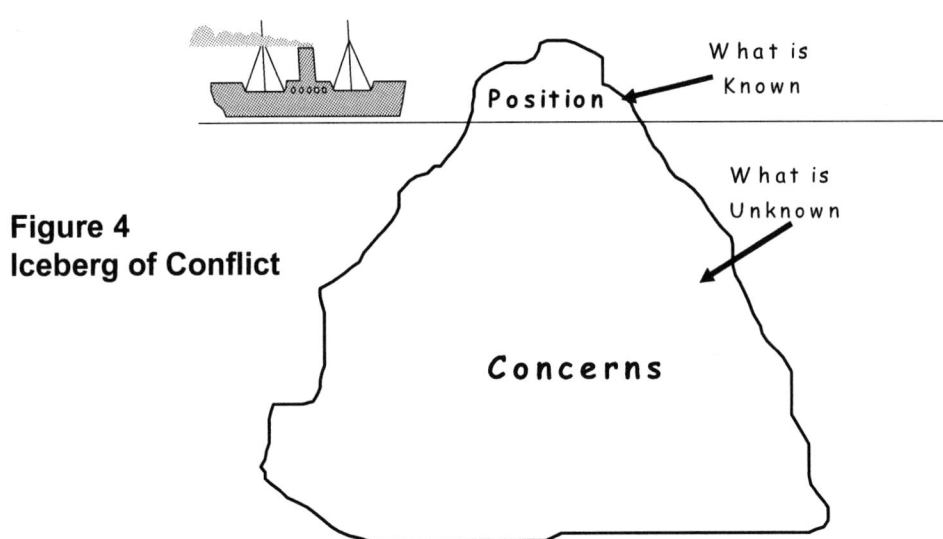

**Figure 4
Iceberg of Conflict**

important and substantial portion of the conflict is often hidden beneath the surface.

Concern

One's position is simply the surface or visible expression of a conflict. One's concerns make up the larger and much less visible need that underlies the position. And as we learned from the Titanic, what is below the surface is far more dangerous that what we see on the surface.

The table below lists a few examples of surface positions and the concerns that might underlie those positions. For example, suppose you are at a social gathering and someone says, "All guns should be outlawed!" Their position is one of gun control. If you were to dig deeper, you would find that their real concern is family safety; something you probably also agree upon.

Position	Concern
Gun Control	Keep family safe
Immigration control	Protect jobs
Allow abortion	Women's right to choice
Get a tattoo	Fit in with my peers

By going beyond the surface reason for a conflict and striving to understand another person's concerns, we can determine why the position matters to them so much. By understanding our concerns, another person can understand the needs that the position satisfies.

In *The Seven Habits of Highly Effective People*, Stephen Covey calls this step, "Seeking first to understand before trying to be understood."[6] Often, individuals in conflict try to resolve the issue while conducting their conversation at a very shallow level. The result is each person presents their personal position without trying to understand the reasoning behind the other person's position.

Without understanding the driving needs behind a particular position, we cannot reach a constructive understanding. When a person consistently uses positive communication skills to ensure they understand another's concerns, they build up a high level of trust with that person.

By understanding one's concerns, we might also find that their suggestion or issue is better than ours, or that the ideas can be combined for an even more synergistic solution. The important thing is that we make our reasoning and needs open and explicit to the other person or group.

Without understanding the driving needs behind a particular position, we cannot reach a constructive understanding.

You should not move to the 'goal' stage until you are both able to articulate the concerns of the other person clearly and to their satisfaction.

Some people believe it is best to keep 'all their cards close to their chest.' Others may not have given much thought to what their needs and reasoning are. Some may be embarrassed to reveal what their needs and reasoning might be. And in any group, there are those individuals who were raised all their lives to share their thoughts and feelings openly, and others who have always been told it is not proper to do so. You can probably see now how important it is to spend some time establishing the principles to guide behavior in situations such as this.

Goal

Once the needs and reasoning of the other person are clearly understood, it is appropriate to move to the Goal stage. Here you want to discover what a true 'win-win' solution would look like to the other person. Sometimes, in a conflict we want to jump directly to telling the other person what we think the solution 'ought to be.' Jumping directly to the goal stage without understanding the other person's concerns may cause the other person to become defensive or feel misunderstood.

During the course of the discussion, you should be attempting to explain how your concerns, or needs, will be achieved if your goal is reached. The other person should be doing the same.

Actions

Most people have some outcomes in mind and appropriate ac tions that they believe will help them fulfill their goals.

It is very important to understand not only another person's concerns and goals, but also what concrete steps they feel will best meet their needs.

Clarifying each others' desired actions are very beneficial because there are almost always many different ways of achieving the same outcome. It is a little like driving from one part of town to another; there are many different routes to arrive at the same destination.

Once two or more individuals have honesty arrived at an understanding of each others' concerns and goals, it is often very easy for them to arrive at action steps that meet the needs of all involved.

Once two or more individuals have honesty arrived at an understanding of each others' concerns and goals, it is often very easy for them to arrive at action steps that meet the needs of all involved.

The Concerns-Goals-Actions (CGA) approach is the cornerstone of the conflict mediation system (Figure 5). When a problem or conflict occurs, the individuals or group members involved begin by working through identification of each others concerns, goals and potential actions. In the next chapter, you will learn specific skills that can be used at each stage of the CGA model to enhance communication.

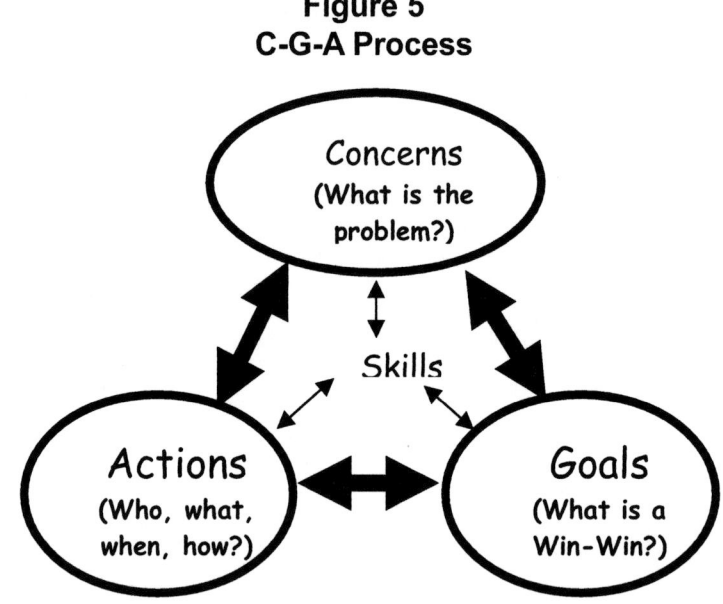

Figure 5
C-G-A Process

Concerns
(What is the
problem?)

Skills

Actions
(Who, what,
when, how?)

Goals
(What is a
Win-Win?)

Case Study #1- Beth and Steve

Identifying another person's concerns, goals and desired actions sounds easy, doesn't it? Let's test your skills by having you view a fairly typical situation in which two individuals have different ideas about how to spend their evening. In the sidebar you will find a case example that describes a situation between two individuals. Start by reading the case example and then answer the questions below:

1.   What is each person's position?

Beth:_____

Steve:_____

2. What might be each person's concerns?

Beth:_____

Steve:_____

Case Example:

Beth has been working late almost every night this whole week. It is finally Friday and she is looking forward to relaxing at home for a change. In fact, Beth picked up a video on the way home that will be perfect for sitting back and letting herself unwind.

As she enters the door, her husband, Steve, greets her with the following news. "Honey, guess what? I made reservations for us to go out to dinner tonight and I bought tickets to the ballet! And don't worry, the sitter will be here in just a few minutes; all you need to do is shower and change. You do need to get moving or we will miss our dinner reservations."

3. What might be each person's goals?

Beth:_____

Steve:_____

4. What actions might meet each person's actions?

Beth:_____

Steve:_____

5. How might Beth and Steve collaborate to resolve this conflict?

Beth:_____

Steve:_____

Let's see how you did. What is each person's position?

The two positions that have been expressed are that one person wants to go out, and one person wants to stay home. **Is this a conflict?** Yes, but in most cases it is not a very serious conflict. However, if not handled tactfully and with care, it could become a much bigger issue than it needs to become.

On the other hand, if each individual takes the time to describe their concerns then both can see that each has good reasons for their positions and do not hold any bad intent. This process may seem very simple, but the more difficult the issue, the more difficult it is to express one's needs and reasoning.

What might be each person's concerns? Beth has had a hard week. She is tired, worn out, and needs time to unwind. For all we know, she also has a lot to do the next day and really must get to bed early. On the other hand, Steve is trying to do something nice for the both of them. He may know that Beth likes the restaurant and wanted to see the ballet. He may recognize that the two of them don't get to go out very often and is proud for taking the initiative to get a sitter.

What might be each person's goals?   Clearly, Beth would probably prefer to stay at home and do nothing. She might want Steve to cancel the sitter, reservations and exchange the tickets for another date. We can presume she also wants to maintain positive relationships with Steve. Steve is probably all set to go out and have some fun anyway. He also wants to maintain positive relationships with Beth.

What actions might meet each person's actions?   If unproductive conflict is their goal, Beth can say, "Oh, alright, I'll go!" If so, she may go out and resent every minute. Steve could say, "Oh Great! I finally try to do something good for us and all you want to do is stay at home. I'll cancel everything and we'll just sit here and do nothing!"

How might Beth and Steve collaborate to resolve this conflict?   There are many options open to resolve this conflict; which one Beth and Steve select depends on their relationship. It may be possible for Steve to cancel all the plans and reschedule them for another weekend. On the other hand, the ballet tickets may be non-refundable and Steve could cancel the dinner reservations and allow Beth time to relax a little before they go to the ballet. Beth might take a quick shower, get dressed and feel like going out after all. Steve may decide to go to dinner and the ballet by himself or with a friend. Note that there are many ways to resolve the conflict.

Case Study #2 – Work Team

This example was between two family members. In the example below, a work group attempts to address a problem that has developed between two members, Julia and Ian. Read through the case and see if you can identify what the position, concerns and goals might be for Julia and Ian. For this case study, you are going to be asked to fill in each person's position, concerns, goals and actions on a worksheet designed to help all members view the conflict holistically.

Julia and Ian are team members working in the same manufacturing area. At their weekly meeting, both announce that they plan on taking vacation for a full week during the same week. During the meeting, Julia says, "I just want everyone to remember that I plan on taking the week of Spring Break off for vacation."

"Yeah, me too," says Ian.

The group process facilitator says, "Remember that we agreed as a group that we can't have two people out on vacation during the same time period. If we do, our production numbers could drop."

Julia shrugs, "Look, I have two kids in grade-school so I have to take that week off. I don't get to see my kids enough anyway and it's the only time I can spend some quality time with them."

"Well, I haven't taken a vacation in two years," says Ian. *"I'm going to college at night and this is the only time that I have a week off."*

"Well, I spoke up first, so I get to go," Julia replies.

"That's not fair Julia," says Ian, *"Schools have other holidays you can take off."*

"Yeah," Julia observes, *"But not a whole week, just a day or so here and there at the end of a weekend. How come you need a whole week?"*

"My parents live in Ohio and it takes longer for me to get there. I haven't seen my family for six years." Ian says, *"You still get to spend time with your kids every weekend."*

Julia shakes her head, *"Sorry, but I'm a single mom. I can't afford to pay for child-care for a whole week while I work. And think about it, do you think my kids will enjoy their vacation if they spend the entire time with a baby-sitter? Sorry, but I spoke up first, so I'm taking vacation."*

"Well," Ian states, *"I'm not waiting another year to see my parents. Besides, it's a stupid rule that two people can't take vacation at the same time."*

Ask yourself, is this a conflict situation? If so, is it between just Julia and Ian, or is this a conflict that the group needs to address?

The answer is, probably all the above. If Julia gets to go on vacation, Ian could hold a grudge against Julia, and a grudge against the team for the rule against two people taking time off. If the decision goes against Julia, she might feel the same way. The conflict is also important to the team because this situation will probably occur again in the future.

When you are ready, turn to page 64 where you will find a copy of CGA Worksheet #1. Imagine how you might view the situation first from the perspective of Julia, Ian and as another team member. Begin by identifying the surface problem the team is facing. Second, fill in the blanks for what you think Julia and Ian's position, concerns, goals and action might be.

Now that you have identified what you think the position, concerns, goals and actions might be for Julia and Ian, complete the next row in the worksheet from the team perspective. Ask, "What is the best answer to this potential conflict for the whole team over the long-term?" When you are finished, compare the concerns, goals and actions you developed with those in the example CGA Worksheet #2 on page 65.

Don't be surprised if you have identified some potential concerns, goals and actions that are not listed on the sample CGA worksheet.

Let's look at just a few of the possible actions that were listed on CGA worksheet #2; these are not listed in any particular order of importance.
.

1.   **One person goes now, and the other goes next year -** In the real world, there may be excellent reasons why there is a policy that only one person can go on vacation at one time. After all, don't forget that the team developed the policy as a group. It may be that only one person gets to go on vacation at a time is the best for the whole team. Guaranteeing that the other person gets to go on vacation next may be the best the team can offer.

2.   **Hire a temporary worker or have team members work overtime -** It is probably worth checking to see if there are funds are available to hire a temporary worker or have another team member work overtime to ensure productivity is achieved. Depending on the level of team autonomy, the team may be able to make this decision, or it may need to negotiate this possibility with management. Maybe this issue has occurred at a time when other team members can cover the absence of two members during regular work hours.

3.   **Revisit the rule -** After considering all the options, the team may find that while the rule made sense in the past, it does not make sense now.

Or, after looking at the facts, the team may find that at certain times of the year, the rule makes sense, but during other times, it does not.

5.   Julia and Ian take vacation, but not the full week - Julia and Ian may decide that to maintain good relations and ensure team productivity, they will each take a few days off at different times during the week.

Case Study # 3 – Your Personal Example

Thus far you have had the opportunity to consider a conflict between two loved ones, and a work team. Now you have a chance to complete CGA Worksheet #3 on a problem that you are facing. As in the work team example above, it is suggested that you following this procedure:

1.   Take a few minutes to identify a conflict in which you are now involved. This could be a conflict at work, between a family member or friend, or a community group or association. To keep it simple, we suggest you keep the number of parties involved to two.

2.   List yourself and the other participants.

3.   Identify the surface problem over which you and the other individual are having conflict. As in the example with Julia and Ian, write this in a way that both you and the other individual would agree upon. (You are not agreeing on how you will resolve the problem, you are just agreeing on the surface description).

4.   Complete the concerns, goals and actions blocks for yourself.

5.   Complete the concerns, goals and action blocks for the other person. Try very hard to be objective and to honestly reflect what you believe how the other person would fill in these blocks.

6.   Look at the information you have completed to determine the following;

        a.   Are you able to understand the other person's concerns or goals better?

        b.   Are there areas of concern or action that provide points from which you might both collaborate to a 'win-win' solution?

As you can see, the CGA model is a very simple, yet powerful method for identifying the key elements that influence the resolution of a potential conflict.

Taking the time to clearly understand what a problem looks like from another's perspective, what a good solution might look like, and what actions might be taken to resolve the problem helps those involved maintain a high level of trust and collaborative problem-solving. In addition, the CGA model addresses these three questions in a way that is simple to remember and apply.

The team's values, safe environment guidelines, communication skills, power management, process leadership, and face-saving techniques should help to guide the discussion. In Chapter 4, you will learn specific skills that can be used at each stage of the CGA model to enhance communication.

---

[6]*Seven Habits of Highly Effective People.* (1989). S. R. Covey. Simon & Schuster, New York.

the CGA model
is a very simple,
yet powerful method
for identifying
the key elements
that influence
the resolution
of a potential conflict.

CGA Worksheet #1 – Julia & Ian

Problem:

Position	Concern	Goal	Actions
Julia			
Ian			
Team			

CGA Worksheet #2 - Julia & Ian

Problem: Two team members want to take vacation at the same time

Position	Concern	Goal	Actions
Julia - Wants to take vacation	• Quality time with kids	• Save money • See kids • Relax, unwind	• Take vacation anyway • Split vacation with Ian
Ian - Also wants to take vacation	• See parents • Parents getting older • Hasn't had vacation in 2 years	• Relax, unwind • See parents	• Take vacation later • Split vacation with Julia
Team – Policy does not permit two people to take vacation at the same time	• Production	• Maintain production & team morale	• One person goes now and one next year • Find a temp • Revisit the policy • Cover for both Julia & Ian

CGA Worksheet #3 – Personal Example

Problem:

Position	Concern	Goal	Actions

Conflict Mediation Skills

Chapter 4

Developing strong, collaborative communication skills is a vital aspect of defining the boundaries for guiding effective group behavior.

In Chapter Three you learned that the Concerns-Goals-Actions (CGA) model is an effective tool for addressing conflict. You also learned that by establishing principles to guide group behavior you can define boundaries of the field and rules to play the game. The CGA model describes the offensive and defensive strategy you will follow in playing the game.

In this chapter, you will learn specific skills that will help achieve your strategy. To help you remember the skills, we will refer to them by the acronym, **CLARC** - for Confront, Listen, Acknowledge, Respond and Commit.

These skills should be used during any stage of the CGA process. One skill is not better than another. Smart players use whichever skills are appropriate for the situation.

Confront

Listen

Acknowledge

Respond

Commit

Confront

Confrontation,
as used here,
means that one or more
of the parties involved
brings a problem
or issue forward
to be collaboratively
examined

Most conflicts escalate because people do not address problems openly and honestly. Instead, many people try to avoid the conflict, and simply allow a problem to grow until it becomes a major issue. Others accommodate or compromise in ways that seem appropriate for the short term, but with which they become increasingly dissatisfied over the long term.

Some people use a competitive approach to get their way through force of personality, position or some other mechanism. This latter approach can be thought of an, "I win-you lose" outcome which will almost always result in a situation that one party strongly resents. If the ultimate result is that one or more individuals fail to fully support the decision, the conflict will usually fester and need to be addressed again at a later date.

In the business environment, conflicts that continually renew themselves are generally a recipe for poor customer service, lowered productivity or efficiency, and declining interpersonal relationships. The only way to consistently achieve positive, constructive results over the long term is by collaborating to identify and resolve current or potential conflicts. The only way to get this process started is to **confront** the issue.

Confrontation is one of those words that can have more than one meaning.

Confrontation is most commonly used or interpreted by people in a negative way. When used from a negative manner, confrontation conveys a hostile or defiant position. Confrontation, as the word is used here, is intended to mean the parties involved bring a problem or issue forward to be collaboratively examined.

The intention is to bring those in conflict face-to-face with the issue or problem. The intent is *not* to throw the problem or issue in the face of the other party involved. Rather, the purpose of confrontation is to make the problem or issue explicit, or observable to everyone.

Interpersonal conflicts always have at least two owners. It might be two or more people or two or more groups. One of the parties may not be aware that they are one of the owners, but at least two people have a stake in the resolution of the conflict.

The best method we have found for confronting a problem or issue between individuals or teams is to use 'I' statements. The purpose of 'I' statements is to ensure that the person who is confronting the other takes ownership of their feelings in a nonthreatening fashion.

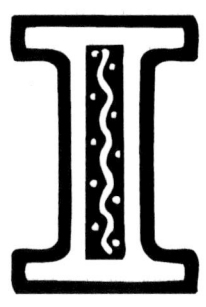

The purpose
of 'I' statements
is to ensure
that the person
who is confronting
the other takes ownership
of their feelings
in a non-threatening
fashion

"I" statements allow you to express your ideas and opinions without blaming the other person.

A complete "I" statement includes four crucial elements:

1. An objective description of the situation or behavior
2. Your personal reaction or feelings
3. The consequences from your perspective
4. Ask how the other party views this issue.

The I statement formula above is illustrated below-

1. When (describe the situation or behavior),
2. I feel (state your personal reaction or feeling)
3. Because (describe the consequences)
4. I'd like to hear how you feel about this issue, What you think, etc.

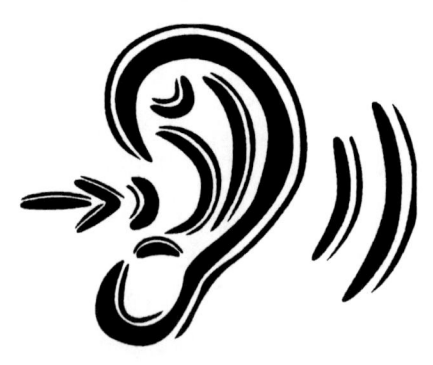

For example, suppose another group member is frequently late for work and you have to cover for them until they arrive. One way to respond might be to say, "Hey look, I'm tired of you coming in late all the time so you better be on time tomorrow!" Even if you are correct, the other person will probably react defensively.

You can confront the other member in a more positive manner using an 'I" statement such as: "When you are late for work, it makes me feel irritated because I have to do my work and your work and the quality of both suffers. How do you see this situation?"

As you can see, in using an "I" statement, you clearly identify what the issue is, how you feel, and what you think the consequences might be from your perspective. This has been achieved in a positive fashion that also allows the other individual to respond.

Using an "I" statement is also a great way to start the CGA process by letting the other person know you have a concern and an indication of what your needs might be; e.g., "I need to focus on doing my work so that the quality does not suffer"..

Now that we have discussed how to confront an issue, we are ready to look at the skill of listening.

…using an "I" statement
clearly identifies the issue,
how you feel,
and what you think
the consequences
might be
from your perspective

Listen

For quality communication to take place it is important that the parties involved listen to each other. Effective listening is a lot more than just avoiding the bad habit of interrupting someone or trying to finish their sentences when they are speaking.

Effective listening also means taking the time to truly pay attention to what the other person feels and wants. It means listening for their reasons, experiences and assumptions so that you understand what thoughts are driving their comments or recommendations. Effective listening is being patient enough to listen to the other person's entire thought rather than waiting impatiently for your chance to respond.

Careful listening is difficult when you have different ideas from others. If you react too quickly to come to a judgment without taking time to understand the other person the chance for defensiveness increases greatly. You want to understand the other person first, but understanding someone does not necessarily mean that you accept their point of view.

When you encounter a different view from your own, follow three simple rules: delay judgment, pay attention to the whole meaning of what is being said, and ask questions to ensure you understand what is being said.

Delaying judgment means that you should not be too quick to criticize what the other person - even in you own head. In the best-seller, *Don't Sweat the Small Stuff... and* it's all small stuff," Richard Carlson[7] observes that when you hurry someone along, interrupt, or finish another person's sentences, you must keep track not only of your own thoughts, but those of the person you are interrupting.

Carlson goes on to note that this style of ineffective listening makes people nervous, causes arguments and resentment. If there is anything really bothers people, it's trying to explain something to another person who is not listening to what you are saying. On the other hand, we all appreciate those individuals whom we feel always take the time to really listen. To build a strong, effective team communication process, each team member must, as Stephen Covey points out, seek first to understand, then to be understood.

The second aspect of listening is to pay attention to the entire meaning of the message. Try to sense the concerns behind what the other individual is expressing. What are the feelings, reasoning, needs and assumptions behind the other person's comments? What are the implications of what is being said not only for the other person, but for you and the rest of the work group?

When encountering differing opinions:

1. Delay judgment
2. Pay attention to meaning
3. Ask questions

To attend effectively, you must consciously slow down your thinking and wait for the other person to finish. It also means that you should pay attention to the other person's body language and tone of speech. People often convey a great deal about their feelings or attitudes by the tone of voice, their posture and or the gestures they use during a conversation.

Finally, ask questions to ensure you understand what is being said. The philosophy behind this point should not be missed: people almost always have good reasons for their opinions. Even if you disagree with the other person's opinion, they will respond much more positively to you if you convey to them that you appreciate their point of view.

When the other individual has completed their point, try to find out as much as you can about their perspective by asking nonjudgmental questions. For example, ask them questions that allow them to clarify:

1.   What happened
2.   Who was involved
3.   How they personally were affected
4.   What they hope to achieve for themselves and for the team with their suggestion

People almost always have good reasons for their opinions. So even if you disagree … they will respond more positively if you appreciate their point of view.

People have been raised differently, have had different experiences and approach life differently. Asking nonjudgmental questions as suggested above allows you to understand how others might come to different suggestions or conclusions than you.

Once you feel that you understood both the content and reasoning behind what another person is saying, you can then acknowledge what you believe you have heard.

Acknowledge

Effective communication is a process of both sending a message and ensuring that it is properly received. It is generally not enough to simply hear what another person is saying.

You may have played the children's game called "Telephone line." In the game, one person tells the next person in line a short message. The second person then repeats the message to the third person and so on until all children involved have 'heard,' and passed on the message. The result is usually that the original and final messages have very little in common. The reason is that each person hears, interprets and re-words the message slightly differently from the person that conveyed the message to them.

Asking nonjudgmental questions allows you to understand how others might come to different suggestions or conclusions than you

Similarly, for your group members to feel that you have truly heard what they have to say, you must accurately acknowledge what you believe they said. Further, they must agree that you heard them correctly.

There are a number of productive ways to acknowledge what you another person have said. **One way is to restate what the other person has said**. A few examples of effective use of restating are illustrated in Figure 6 on page 77.

You can also acknowledge what another person has said in a constructive manner by reframing. Reframing helps to soften and neutralize hostile comments and encourages forward movement by clarifying thoughts or introducing creative possibilities. Some examples of reframing are illustrated in Figure 7 on page 78.

These are just a few suggestions for ensuring that you acknowledge what another person has said in a way that allows them to correct you if needed. By acknowledging in this manner, you can ensure that what you thought you heard is not what the other person really said.

Figure 6
Restatement Examples

What to Restate	Example
Main points the other person made	"So your biggest concern is making sure everyone has an important role on the team?"
Important details raised	"You're saying the budget allows us to increase our recognition fund by 10% next year?"
Comments that might help the team to move forward	"It sounds like you are suggesting we put partitions on the manufacturing floor to provide teams a place to meet that is a little quieter."
Information that you may not have quite understood	"Let's see, you're saying you want every other Tuesday & Thursday off from 2-4 PM to attend a community college course. Is that right?"
Comments or suggestions when you think the other person may not feel they were understood by you or heard by others on the team	"Jean, did you just say that we come up for an audit review next month?"

Figure 7
Reframing Examples

What to reframe	Example
From past to future	A team member says, "I am getting sick and tired of all these absences! We can't get any work done!" **Reframe**: "So you want to see attendance improved in the future, is that right?"
From negative to positive	A co-worker says, "This 12 hour shift is too much." **Reframe:** "It sounds like you want to find a way to make the work shift more tolerable."
From personal attack to problem definition	An employee says, If that secretary forgets to give me my messages one more time I am going to scream." **Reframe:** "Are you saying that we need to find a better method of ensuring messages get passed along?"
From a demand to a goal	A co-worker says, "I want a private office so I can get away from all these distractions!" **Reframe:** "You need a way to get your work done without distractions?"

Figure 7
Reframing Examples (continued)

From an individual concern to a team concern	A team member says, "I had so much to do I couldn't monitor the equipment until after 3 PM." **Reframe:** "It sounds like we need to work out a way to make sure someone can monitor the equipment on a regular basis."
From a concern to action	A manager says, "We waste too much time in these meetings and nothing gets done!" **Reframe:** "You want to have a more efficient agenda?"

Respond

The **CLARC** skills you have learned so far include how to confront the other person to make a problem or issue explicit in a way that does not cause a defensive reaction. You have also learned how to listen so that the other person feels he or she has your attention. Third, you have learned how to acknowledge what you have heard. Again, you are not agreeing with the other person, simply ensuring that what was said is what you heard.

The fourth of the CLARC skills is respond.

One can respond in two different ways. First, you can respond to gather additional information and to better understand perspectives, feelings, concerns or needs. Second, you may respond to give your reply, answer or reaction to what the other person is saying.

Ideally, when you respond to someone do so in a way that allows for a common, open and free exchange of ideas and thoughts so that you are able to build the conversation in a positive way. You should avoid responding to someone in a way that closes the door on the discussion or 'puts-down' what was said. For example, giving a flat response of 'no' closes the door on a conversation. Saying, 'yes, but…," is a negative response as you are saying, "Yes, I heard you, but I don't agree." This is the same thing as saying 'no.'

To encourage additional information, perspective, feelings, or concerns it is better to respond in a way that conveys that you are open-minded, respectful, and willing to explore options. Ask open-ended questions that request additional information, a different perspective, exploration of alternatives, and so on. Figure 8 on page 81 lists a number of ways that you can respond to encourage the conversation.

How have you seen others respond that caused defensiveness?

_____

_____

_____

_____

_____

Figure 8
Responding Examples

1. What would it look like if...?
2. What would have to happen to make your suggestion possible?
3. What would need to change...?
4. Who is a good model of...?
5. What works best when...?
6. Can you tell me about a time when what you are suggesting went just right?
7. What have we done that has worked well before?
8. How do you think this impacts the team (or another unit)?

Can you think of other ways to respond that will encourage conversation?

_____

_____

_____

_____

_____

_____

_____

These responses are just examples, of course. You can modify them or add any other similar type of response that helps to foster effective communication.

For example, let's say that another employee approaches you and says, "I am so tired of trying to work with Bob. I asked him three times where the file was and he continued to look out the window as if I wasn't even there!"

One way to respond might be to say, "Yes, isn't he a loser?" Doing so however, does not build the strength of the group or resolve this situation. A better response might be to say, "What have you done in the past that was successful at getting Bobs attention?"

Something to consider is that if you respond in a negative manner about another person, the individual with whom you are speaking may well wonder what you say about them when they are not around.

The second way to respond is to share your reaction or feelings about what someone else has suggested. You have already learned one effective method is to use "I" statements. Remember that a good "I" statement identifies what the issue is, how you feel and what you think the consequences are from your perspective. The purpose of a good "I" statement is to respond in a positive fashion that also allows the other individual to respond in kind.

For example, in a team meeting, someone might be suggesting a new method for orienting new members to the work environment. You might say, "Ted, if I understood you correctly, you are suggesting that we each spend one hour with each new team member to explain our role on the team. I like that idea because when we take the time to explain what we

Something to consider is that if you respond in a negative manner about another person, the individual with whom you are speaking may well wonder what you say about them when they are not around

do to new members, they are able to become fully performing team members sooner." In this example, we combined the acknowledgment skill with a response using an "I" statement.

Commit

A major source of conflict between group members occurs when they fail to commit to some action or next steps. Group members should commit when they are satisfied that the present item or suggestion under discussion has been sufficiently covered to move on.

Sometimes, people enter into a discussion, agree on the cause of a conflict or the necessary solution, but stop without defining a next step. When this happens, people may leave with different and perhaps contradictory ideas of what a solution might be, when it might happen and who will address the problem. Worse yet, if someone leaves the discussion feeling that their interests or needs are not fully understood, they may sabotage the effort in some way.

To avoid a conflict due to lack of commitment, it is important to spell out who, what, when, where, how and why. By defining 'who,' the team is ensuring that accountability is clear. By discussing 'what,' you are clarify-

To avoid a conflict
due to lack
of commitment,
it is important
to spell out who, what,
when, where, how
and why

ing the actual action or steps the individual who is accountable will take.

'When' defines the time frame within which the action or steps will be taken. **'Where,'** if appropriate, makes the physical location or setting explicit. By defining **'how,'** you are identifying any resource or procedural needs or limitations. Finally, explaining **'why,** ensures that the reason for investing the time and energy is clear. **'Why,'** also explains why it is important to the group.

Using the CLARC Skills

Knowing the **CLARC** skills is one thing. Using them on a daily basis is another. As indicated at the beginning of this chapter, any skill or combination of skills should be used when appropriate.

When trying to resolve a conflict, it may be necessary to confront the problem, listen to what the other person has to say, acknowledge, listen more, respond, listen more, respond, acknowledge, respond and then commit. You may revisit a skill several times during the course of a conversation. It is important that you should commit before leaving the topic.

Confront

Listen

Acknowledge

Respond

Commit

[1] Don't Sweat the Small Stuff, Richard Carlson, (1997, Hyperion, New York.

Third Party Mediation

Chapter 5

*L*inda is the Executive Director of a nonprofit center serving low income families in a large community. *She and her staff have been very busy over the past week preparing for the end-of-year Board meeting to review goals and strategies for the coming year. As she is reviewing her notes, Robert, one of the more vocal and influential members of the Board sticks his head in the door.*

"Hi Linda," he says cheerily, "Mind if I have a quick word with you?"

"Sure, what's up?" she replies, motioning him to a seat.

"Well, as you know we will be reviewing what you have planned for the coming year in next week's Board meeting. I believe, and I think you will certainly agree that it is vital that we broaden our services to include homeless families." He pauses and looks at her, "You do think this is an important service don't you?"

"That is certainly one of the services we should be considering," Linda replies noncommittally.

"Then to get straight to the point, Margaret Morris the Board co-chair and I disagree on this topic. I am convinced that expanding our services to the homeless is the right thing to do and Margaret is just being stubborn and obstinate about this opportunity. I think it is important that you take a strong stand in the Board meeting so that she will understand that this is the right thing to do. Can I count on you to back me up?"

This scenario illustrates a fundamental dynamic that is reenacted between individuals in businesses, not-for-profits, universities, associations and governmental institutions worldwide on a daily basis. Subordinates, co-workers or associates often approach someone else with their view of a problem or solution and try to enlist them as supporters.

Given her position, it would not be prudent for Linda to 'buy-into' Roberts request for her support for several reasons:

First, this is a no-win situation. If Linda agrees to support Robert, she will alienate Margaret. If she supports Margaret, she alienates Robert.

Second, Linda does not know why Robert and Margaret feel they way they do. Referring back to the CGA model, the only thing she can identify is Robert's position.

Subordinates, coworkers
or associates
often approach someone
else with their view
of a problem or solution
and try to enlist them
as supporters.

Third, taking sides or trying to solve the conflict herself will not help Robert and Margaret work more effectively together. The Board members must be able and willing to work through conflicts so that they can best advise Linda on how to help the organization succeed.

The good news is that managers and teams skilled in the conflict mediation system may choose alternative methods for resolving conflicts that threaten to derail productivity. In this chapter, we describe how Linda can serve as a third party mediator and coach Robert to a positive resolution of his conflict with Margaret.

Third Party Mediation

A third party mediator is a neutral individual who helps others in conflict to bring to the surface and discuss their concerns, goals, and potential actions. A third party mediator may be another group member, the team leader, a manager, an individual from another unit or someone from outside the organization altogether.

When individuals are skilled in the conflict mediation, they are usually able to resolve most routine conflicts that arise. However, there will be occasions when a third party mediator may be necessary.

A third party mediator
is a neutral individual
who helps others
bring to the surface
and discuss
their concerns, goals,
and potential actions

A third party mediator may be needed when one or more of the participants has become so emotionally engaged that they cannot separate themselves from the problem and potential solutions. Disagreements or misunderstandings may grow to a point that the conflict threatens unity or relationships with others.

If the conflict is not surfaced and resolved, individuals may begin to let the problem worsen, avoid dealing with it and/or begin attacking each other overtly or covertly. Stress, tension and bad feelings escalate and continue to hinder productivity and a positive working environment.

The second occasion a third party mediator may be needed is when an individual or group is faced with a problem that is beyond their scope of responsibility, knowledge or resources to address. All individuals, teams and organizations have limits or boundaries on knowledge, skills, roles, responsibilities, budgets, time, organizational policies and resources. When limits are reached, it is necessary to request assistance from another person or source to resolve the problem.

Use of a third party mediator is normal and should not be looked upon as a 'failure' of the participants. It is important to recognize that human beings do get emotionally invested in their positions and they do

Use of a third party mediator is normal and should not be looked upon as a 'failure' of the participants

reach limits on authority and resources. When either occasion occurs, it is wise to rely on a third party mediator.

Ideally, the individual selected to serve as the third party mediator should be skilled in conflict mediation process and the **CLARC** skills. They should also be models of strong process leadership which is important for keeping the team members on track, focused and operating within the guidelines of behavior and expectations previously identified by the team.

Third party mediation may take a number of forms depending on the nature of the problem. The two most common forms of mediation assistance is to ask or appoint a team member to serve as team process mediator during each team meeting or to request assistance from the team leader or manager. On other occasions, it may make more sense to request a mediator from outside the team or unit.

Regardless of who is selected or chooses to play the mediator role, the individual serving as the process leader must remain true to the role of keeping the team on track. The mediator should keep the individuals or team members focused on the agenda, and ensure that all members are:

Third party mediation may take a number of forms depending on the nature of the problem

1.   Adhering to the operating framework
2.   Following the CGA process
3.   Using the CLARC skills

The process mediator needs to remain neutral regarding the issue even if they are going to be affected by the outcome. On occasion, the process mediator may need to 'change hats,' and explicitly step out of their role in order to provide their input to the discussion. When this situation occurs, the process mediator should stop the discussion and ask someone else to serve as mediator while he or she shares their thoughts, feelings or suggestions. As soon as the individual has shared their thoughts, feelings or suggestions, they can retake the role of process mediator.

Most conflicts occur between two or more individuals within an organization. Once in a while, two individuals may reach a point where they cannot move ahead constructively. When this occurs, the individuals involved can approach another individual on the team who is not affected by the issue to serve as a third party process mediator. In these situations, the same guidelines pertain to a mediator between two individuals as to a process mediator for a group. The process mediator should keep the group focused on the agenda and ensure that all members are adhering to the principles and values described within the group operating framework,

The process mediator
needs to remain neutral
regarding the issue
even if they are going
to be affected
by the outcome

following the CGA process, and using the **CLARC** skills. Usually, an individual in this role will not need to interject any comments or suggestions of their own.

Coaching Those In Conflict

It is not uncommon for an employee to approach another employee with the intention of getting support for their cause. People can avoid being co-opted into either taking sides, or 'solving' the problem if they simply coach the inquiring individual through the CGA process.

Recall the scenario at the beginning of this chapter. Robert stopped in Linda's office complaining of a conflict with another Board member. Further, he has explicitly asked for Linda to support him and not Margaret. What should Linda do now?

Assume that the Board and staff of Linda's organization have been trained in this conflict mediation process. During the training, they would have reviewed or developed the principles that outline their values, roles, and methods of communication. These principles would also describe the way they care to interact and the outcomes they hope to attain.

simply coach
the inquiring individual
through the CGA process

Let's see how Linda might respond in such a way as to be respectful of both Margaret and Robert, while not taking responsibility for solving the problem.

"Let me make sure I understand what you're saying Robert," said Linda after Robert finished. "You feel that it is important that we broaden our services to include homeless families, is that right?"

"That is exactly what I am saying," Robert responded
.

Linda went on, "And Margaret does not share your view on this issue, is that right?"

"No, as I said, she is being obstinate and just can't seem to see why this would be so valuable to the agency," said Robert.

"So the problem seems to be that you and Margaret disagree on the issue of whether to serve homeless families during the upcoming year. Am I saying this correctly?" stated Linda.

Robert leaned forward, "Linda, that's what I've been saying. Now I need you to straighten Margaret out once and for all so we can get this issue behind us and work on other more important issues."

"Have you asked Margaret how she sees the problem, what her concerns are on this issue or explained yours to her," Linda inquired.

"Well," Robert said slowly, "No, I haven't had the chance, but it's no use; she has already made up her mind."

"Even if she has, shouldn't you two be working together to share what you hope to see for the coming year, why you feel the way you do and what actions might get us there?" said Linda. "Let me suggest this; suppose you set up a time to meet with Margaret for you two to talk about this issue. If you think she will be resistant, what could you do that might help her share her thoughts?"

Robert moved in his seat, "I guess I could see if she agrees on the problem and then let her share her concerns first."

"What will you do next," Linda prompted.

Robert smiled and said, "Okay, okay, I can share my concerns and then we can both share what actions we think are possible and what our visions might look like."

"Great, after you are done, come back and let me know how it went," Linda said as she stood up to shake Robert's hand and escort him to the door.

What happened in this interchange between Linda and Robert?

First, Linda did not respond to Robert's immediate request that she support him in strong-arming Margaret. Rather, she made sure she understood the problem as defined by Robert. (Margaret is not there, so Linda made no attempt to suggest she understood Margaret's point of view). Once Robert had confirmed that she understood the problem from his viewpoint, she then asked if he understood how Margaret's saw the problem and her concerns. When Robert said that he had not talked with Margaret on this issue, Linda suggested he do so. Note that she did not offer to be there too. Remember that the goal of this process is to solve the conflict at the lowest possible level.

It is also important to observe that Linda has modeled the **CLARC** skills. Linda has clarified Roberts' view of the situation, paraphrased to ensure understanding and acknowledged his feelings.

But suppose Robert said he feels uncomfortable with the meeting or doesn't know what to say to Margaret?   Linda's role now is to coach him to be able to take that step himself. Consider the following:

Robert leaned back and sighed, "Linda that all sounds great, but I really don't know what Margaret and I would have to talk about."

"Okay," said Linda, "How could you find out how she sees the problem or what problem she feels is more important?"

"I guess I could ask her what her concerns are regarding homeless families," Robert said.

Linda persisted, "Then what?"

"I could tell her why I think homeless families are a problem and explain my concerns," he replied, "But what if she just disagrees with me? Aren't we right back to square one?"

"Good point, if she sees the problem differently than you, she probably will disagree," Linda agreed, "But what are you going to do if and when that happens? Isn't it important that you two work through this together?"

"Yeah," he said.

"Suppose you map out the problem, your concerns, vision and actions and share those with her up front." Linda prompted.

"You mean lay my cards on the table, just like that?" Robert said raising his eyebrows.

"Yes, and ask her to do the same."

"Well, I can do that but it sounds too simple to resolve our disagreement," complained Robert.

"You're right, it may not resolve the disagreement," Linda said nodding, *"But what will this do for both of you?"*

Robert sighed again, *"It will help us understand where each other are coming from and why."*

"Right!" replied Linda. *"Now, when are you going to arrange the meeting with her? Do you want to use my phone?"*

As in the first interchange, Linda has used effective listening skills and avoided taking on the responsibility of solving the conflict between Robert and Margaret. Instead, she has coached him through his own doubts and helped him consider several actions he can take.

First she helped him consider how he might approach Margaret by asking for her view first. Second, Linda suggested he map out the CGA process from his viewpoint and share it with Margaret. Third, she suggested he take action by using her phone and arranging the meeting right away. Linda could take the process one step farther by asking him to follow up with her and share the results of the meeting.

Does this mean the coaching is over? No, it simply means Linda has helped Robert take the next step. She can provide additional coaching or actually get involved as a mediator if necessary.

Direct Mediation

Now that you have seen how an individual can coach another to take responsibility and action for resolving their own conflict, **let's see how someone might play a direct role as a mediator.** Consider the role Linda might play if Robert and Margaret return and request Linda mediate their conflict.

Linda is standing at a flip chart diagramming her presentation to the Board when she hears a knock on the door. She turns and sees both Robert and Margaret at the door.

"Sorry to interrupt Linda," Margaret says, "But Robert and I are stuck on a major issue and we need your help. Do you have a minute?"

an individual
can coach another
to take responsibility
and action
for resolving
their own conflict

Fortunately, Linda is wrapping up her presentation notes and says, "I'd be glad to help. What can I do?"

"Well," Robert says, "As you and I discussed, I arranged a meeting with Margaret to discuss our views on the homeless family issue. However..."

"What Robert is trying to say," Margaret interjected, "Is that we can't seem to get anywhere taking with each other. Robert just can't seem to understand why focusing on the homeless this year is just out of the question!"

"Robert, Margaret, I am more than willing to help you discuss this, but first I need to remind you both of our operating values," Linda said.

"Operating values?" Robert and Margaret both said at the same time.

Linda walked over to her wall and pointed to a framed drawing. "Remember our Board retreat this past summer? We spend two days laying out the vision for our agency, defining what kind of working environment and relationships we want, laying out our personal and collective values, practicing communication skills, AND," Linda paused significantly, "learning how to resolve conflicts."

Robert nodded, "Oh yeah, I remember that."

"Yes that was a great retreat," observed Margaret.

Linda as she began to draw a CGA matrix on a blank piece of flipchart paper. "Do you two still feel that the work we did and the agreements we developed are important and worth following?"

"Sure," they both said looking at each other.

"Great, do you remember how to fill out this CGA matrix?"

"Of course," said Margaret, "'C' stands for Concerns, 'G' for Goals and 'A' is Accomplishment."

"Well, close," laughed Linda, "'A' is for Action. Okay, let's agree on the problem first."

"I think the problem we should focus upon is whether we should provide services for homeless families in the coming year," said Robert, "Would you agree with that Margaret?"

"Yes, that seems to be the problem we are discussing right now," she answered.

"Okay, so I will write that down as the problem. Now, Robert, what are your concerns about serving homeless families?"

Robert shrugged, "A couple of things. First, with the downturn in the economy, the unemployment rate has risen almost four percent. Many of those people have been thrown out of work and are losing their homes because they can't pay their mortgage or rent payments. While most will find some kind of work, we don't have enough shelter space or resources to feed those who need additional time and assistance."

"What are your concerns regarding the homeless Margaret?" inquired Linda as she listed Roberts points on the CGA matrix.

"First, I agree that the economy has been bad and unemployment is way up," Margaret countered. "But I think our most important priority should be on educating the homeless so they can get jobs. We should be educating these people so they can learn a new skill or trade that is in demand and don't need assistance at all. Then we won't have to put investments in shelters that we may not need again."

"So your concern is that the homeless be educated to take high demand jobs. Is that right?" Linda summarized.

"Yes," Margaret nodded.

"I wonder if there is a way to provide temporary assistance to those who have been laid off and are now homeless while providing educational benefits at the same time," Linda asked.

"I have not really considered that, but I suppose it's possible. I'd have to give it some thought," said Margaret.

Robert nodded thoughtfully, *"I really had not thought about that either. But there are probably some parallel needs."*

"I think so too," said Linda. *"But I have to go to a staff meeting. Suppose I leave you two here with the flipchart and I'll come back when our meeting is done in an hour? Can you two map out some of the possibilities?"*

"Sure," said Robert, *"But I'm not saying this issue is resolved, I'm just saying there might be some overlap."*

"Neither am I," said Margaret.

"Fine, you two get as far as you can and I'll check back with you in an hour," Linda said as she headed for the door.

In the example above, Linda has taken a more active role as a mediator. The interchange between Margaret and Robert began with some snide remarks, so Linda reminded them of their operating values. Once they had agreed on the values, Linda was able to begin by getting both to agree on the problem. She then had them describe their respective concerns.

It is important to note that Linda actually mapped the problem and concerns on the flipchart. She could have illustrated the CGA process on a blackboard, whiteboard or even a piece of paper. The important element is that the process be written down so all involved could see what was being shared.

Remember that Linda's goal is to coach Margaret and Robert to their own resolution of the conflict. In this scenario, once the two Board members seemed to reach some agreement on how their concerns might overlap, Linda took the opportunity to turn the process over to them. She could have stayed and helped them work through the entire CGA process. Since both Robert and Margaret are skilled communicators and at some level of agreement on their concerns, it does not hurt to let them continue. Linda did make a point of saying she would return in one hour to see how they were doing. If they are still stuck, she can coach them both again. **If they are well on their way to resolving the conflict, she need only**

congratulate them.

These scenarios are helpful from several perspectives. While Linda happens to be the executive director of a nonprofit, you can see how the skills she utilized could be applied by anyone. Linda could just as easily been described as an administrative assistant, a manager, a work team member, a real estate broker or any other position. Robert and Margaret did not have to be Board members; they could have been co-workers, managers, vendors or customers. The application of the CLARC skills and CGA process would have been identical in any situation.

First you ensure everyone is clear on the operating values.
Second, model the CLARC skills.
Third, gain agreement on the problem.
Fourth, map out the CGA process, and finally follow-up.

In the next chapter you will learn how the conflict mediation process can be implemented within your organization.

---

[7] *"Don't Sweat the Small Stuff...and it's all small stuff.* (1997). R. Carlson, Ph.D., Hyperion Publishing, New York.

Notes

Managing Conflict In Your Organization

Chapter 6

A major advantage of the conflict mediation system is that it is easily customizable for any organization or unit within that organization. It is flexible enough to be integrated into existing training programs or serve as a stand-alone workshop by itself.

This chapter will describe the various ways that the process can be implemented within an organization. The steps taken to plan and integrate this process into the organization will probably be slightly different; but these guidelines should make the work a little easier.

Value of Customization

E very organization and most units within an organization feel they are different, even unique. As you learned in Chapter 2, defining the principles for defining conduct and behavior is a very important. Ideally, executives, management, employees, team members, asso-

Every organization
and most units
within an organization
feel they are different,
even unique

ciates and/or Board members will work collaboratively to come to an agreement of the principles which will guide conduct and behavior. How this process is implemented within an organization may take various forms.

It may be that the organization implements this process company-wide. It may be that the division or geographical site at which you work decides to implement the process on a more local level. A single department may also decide to implement the process. Any approach can be effective.

Customization Process

The suggested process for customizing and implementing this process in an organization is illustrated in Figure 9 on page 107. Each of its ten steps will be discussed in more detail in this chapter..

Step One: Form Design Team

There are two reasons most conflict mediation training programs are not successful. First, many rely on an external mediator to help the disputing parties to resolve their conflict. It may be appropriate to have a couple of umpires on the field during a football game to resolve conflicts, or to have professional mediators for some human resource disputes, but it is not very practical for minor conflicts in the workplace.

Most conflict mediation training programs are not successful

Figure 9
Customization Process

Step One:	**Form Design Team**
Step Two:	**Determine Principles**
Step Three:	**Identify Training Needs**
Step Four:	**Develop Roll-out Plan**
Step Five:	**Pilot & Improve Training**
Step Six:	**Implement**
Step Seven:	**Monitor & Communicate Results**

Second, few people actually apply the skills they learn in most conflict management training programs. Unlike other conflict management training programs, the conflict mediation system is a culture-change effort. The expressed intention is to establish a culture and environment where managers and employees apply the skills of conflict mediation themselves.

Establish a culture and environment where managers and employees apply the skills of conflict mediation themselves

For this reason, it is recommended that a team of individuals be tasked with planning how the steps for implementing and sustaining the process company-wide should be carried out and by whom. Tasking a team with the responsibility of implementing this process suggests that there should be someone who acts as the sponsor of this effort. That may be the CEO, another executive or someone else with the authority to provide the team with the resources and support it needs to succeed.

In small organizations, it may be that the Design Team is only two or three individuals. In large organizations, it may be wise to select representatives from several areas such as manufacturing, design, sales, marketing, human resources, finance, information technology and the legal departments. The important point is that those who are responsible for ensuring the implementation within your organization be seen as credible and capable of seeing the project through to completion.

Step Two: Determine Principles

Once the team has been convened, their first task is to determine the principles and boundaries that make the best sense for their organization. If an organization has determined that a process for mediating conflict will add significantly to organizational and employee productivity, morale, profitability and/or levels of customer service- certain conditions

**The important point
is that those
who are responsible
for ensuring
implementation
within your organization
be seen as credible
and capable
of seeing the project
through to completion**

must be established. Principles and boundaries offer organizations a method for enabling managers, employees, work units and teams to function effectively and collaboratively over the long-term.

In our experience, there are at least six foundational elements define the 'path' that organization and team members should agree are best for a productive, collaborative, empowering work environment.

1.   **Establish operating values** - Recall that values tell us of what to do and what not to do. Values become the standards of our actions and behaviors, our attitudes towards others and how we treat other people. The organization may already have a clearly articulated set of values. If not, the team needs to develop values that all employees or members can support.

Developing values is not a simple or easy process. The team should consider a number of questions when determining their values such as"
   a.   What do we stand for?
   b.   What behaviors would illustrate what we stand for?
   c.   How do we want to treat each other, our customers and suppliers?

Principles
and boundaries
offer organizations
a method
for enabling managers,
employees, and teams
to function effectively
and collaboratively
over the long-term

d.   How do we want to be seen by the community?

e.   What attitudes and behaviors do we want to recognize and reward?

The answers to these questions should lead the team to identify a number of key values. This list of values will probably be different for every organization. The team can then define the values and share them with focus groups of other employees to obtain their review and suggestions for improvement. Once the list is complete, it should be communicated widely along with examples of behaviors that exemplify each value.

2.   **Create a safe environment** - High performing organizations create environments where members are skilled at communicating with each other about thoughts, ideas and conflicts without resorting to ridicule or competition. This level of work environment is achieved by valuing confidentiality, establishing a mediation system, and by using communication that does not naturally place priority on assigning blame or guilt for conflicts and disputes. The design team should take a critical look at what behaviors and practices exist within the organization that detracts from a safe environment. There may be policies, procedures, unclear roles or responsibilities, abusive personalities that lead to conflict and turmoil.

3.   **Collaborative communication skills** - Effective communication is a very important skill for effective work between the organization, management and employees. While many of us have received training in public speaking, few of us have received training in listening skills. Effective communication is both listening *and* speaking. It may be that your organization needs to implement training opportunities for individual members that provide them with the skills they need to present their ideas and suggestions effectively and then listen appropriately to others.

The **CLARC** skills are based on effective listening and speaking skills and can serve as an effective basis from which to design and/or implement your communication skills training programs.

4.   **Power management** - As was stated in Chapter 2, there are very real differences in power between people and hierarchies within organizations. Executives, management and other organization members must be able to recognize, acknowledge and apply their differences in status, authority, responsibility, expertise, competency, and personality to drive organizational improvement. In so doing, organizations and the individuals within those organizations feel empowered to share the full extent of their knowledge and skills to resolve problems.

Effective communication
is both listening
and speaking

How power is managed within an organization is a clear reflection of its culture. This means the design team must pay close attention to understanding how decisions get made; who makes them and why. They can then consider if the existing power management structure is appropriate or if changes need to be made in policies or procedures that reward different behaviors.

5. **Process leadership** - Individuals working together need to learn how to study a problem, lay out solutions, reach a common decision and take action. If not already in place, it is highly recommended that training be provided to develop a cadre of skilled process facilitators throughout the organization. These would be individuals who learn how do facilitate meetings and apply tools such as force-field analysis, flow-charting, fishbone and affinity diagrams and multi-voting.

Remember that selecting a person to serve as a process facilitator does not necessarily imply any power to the person other than they are to focus on managing the conflict mediation process by clarifying communication, preventing miscommunication and assisting the group in the application of appropriate problem-solving and decision-making methods.

Individuals working together need to learn how to study a problem, lay out solutions, reach a common decision and take action

Step Three: Identify Training Needs

Training in conflict mediation skills is often provided to the following groups:

1.   **All Employees** - Because this is an effort to build conflict management into the entire culture of the organization, all employees, managers and executives should receive the basic training. We have found that the process and skills can be learned within a day or two. If individual units or divisions want to map out their own operating framework, this process can take longer.

2.   **Managers, Team Leaders and Facilitators** - After attending the basic training, those who are managers, team leaders or have been identified as facilitators need to attend training that will give the skills to coach others. This training involves providing these individuals with a clear understanding of their role in leading others to resolve conflicts themselves, serving as mediators in small and large group situations and modeling the CLARC communication skills. It is not uncommon for these individuals to be asked to conduct all or portions of the basic all-employee training. This level of training can typically be learned within a day.

In the process of mapping out the principles, the design team may also identify additional skills and knowledge that are necessary for the process to be totally effective. These could include skills in making presentations to others, meeting management, problem-solving, coaching and team building.

If the organization has skilled curriculum design staff who can integrate these programs into the organization's culture, training can be developed in house. Other organizations find it is easier to simply purchase the training materials for one or both programs. These training materials may be obtained in a generic format or customized specifically for the organization.

We have found that the training can be conducted by both internal and external facilitators. Many organizations find it is best to have an internal instructor co-facilitate with an external trainer. The external trainer brings deep knowledge and experience in group conflict mediation and can share perspectives from many different organizations and workgroups. The internal facilitator provide clear guidance to how the process is applied and sustained within the organization, as well as practical on-the job successes and challenges.

Training
can be conducted
by both internal
and external facilitators

Step Four : Develop Roll-Out Plan

Great training and a great operating framework does not mean you will have great success. For the process to succeed there needs to be a well thought-out plan for rolling it out. Considerations may include:

1.   How will the effort be communicated ahead of time?
2.   Which groups will be trained first? Second?
3.   How many training sessions will be needed?
4.   When and where will the training be held?
5.   Who will provide the training?
6.   What support materials will participants receive during training?
7.   What support will units & teams receive from mediators over time?
8.   What policies, procedures or other organizational systems or processes must be modified, eliminated or developed to sustain the effort?
9.   How will new employees be oriented to this process?

Step Five: Pilot & Improve Training

For medium and large organizations, it is wise to test the training programs on a sample group of executives, managers and employees. The purpose of the pilot is to obtain reactions, identify areas for improving the curriculum and facilitation, logistics, communications and support needed to sustain the training on the job.

There needs to be a well thought-out plan for rolling out your program

Once the pilot has been completed, the design team should oversee any improvements needed to ensure the knowledge and skills to be learned are easily and effectively transmitted to future participants. Changes may also be needed to the way the material is facilitated, location of the training programs, and program length.

If the design team has determined that it is best to have internal staff conduct or co-facilitate the training programs these individuals need to be trained. Most often, train-the-trainer programs follow a process of the individual first attending the basic training as a participant. After attending as a participant, the individual may observe a workshop to take notes, or if they are skilled enough, simply jump to co-facilitating a workshop with a skilled presenter. The final step is to take the lead role as facilitator with a skilled presenter as backup.

Step Six: Implement

After any needed improvements have been made to the curriculum, audio-visual aids, training methods and so on, it is time for the training to be implemented. We strongly suggest that organizations take a top-down approach meaning that executives and managers attend the basic and higher level training first. The advantage of this approach is that these individuals have a great deal of influence on how successfully the effort is perceived and applied in the workplace. By attending the training first, they are not only able to describe and communicate the purpose of the training, but its integration with the organization's culture. Employees also see the training as important if management has made a point of attending first.

The design team will have to work closely with the training, support and operations staff to arrange for an effective roll-out of the training programs. If not accomplished earlier, the design team will need to identify which groups are trained, in what order, when, where and by whom. There may also be a need to ensure that attendance and completion be documented. These are all tasks that the consultants or training staff can facilitate.

Step Seven: Monitor and Communicate Results

Providing the training is not the final step. It is important for the design team to monitor the training process in order to review participant evaluations and recommend additional improvements. As the organization and participants gain experience they will almost certainly discover ways of customizing the training to their organization and the audience. These may include new and better ways of teaching the skills, sharing case studies or examples and presenting the material to enhance participant learn-

Providing the training is not the final step

ing. **Facilitators and management will learn better ways of implementing and coaching others on the job.** By monitoring both the training and its transfer to the workplace, the design team can ensure that the curriculum is constantly updated and refreshed to drive increased application and productivity.

The purpose of the conflict mediation process is to add significantly to organizational and employee productivity, morale, profitability and/or levels of customer service. In the process of mapping out the operating framework, the design team should have identified what kinds of outcomes to expect. Will the number of reported conflicts go down? Will retention improve? Will employees report higher levels of morale and confidence in voicing their opinion? Will service levels or quality improve? Will cycle time decrease along with levels of scrap or errors?

Facilitators and management will learn better ways of implementing and coaching others on the job

A major factor in the ongoing success of this process is to communicate those successes and reward the individuals or groups who were responsible. Communication channels may include organizational, newsletters, staff meetings, special recognition events, e-mails and bulletin boards. The important point is that the communication should be clear, frequent and describe how the ability to mediate conflicts effectively has improved morale, interpersonal relationships, retention and productivity.

A group of pre-teens playing a game in a school yard understand the value of defining the area of play, the rules of the game, their respective roles and responsibilities for playing effectively and what it means to 'win.'

If children can recognize these concepts and implement them effectively isn't it reasonable that those of us in formal organizations or associations should be as well? This mediation process provides an organization with the framework and skill sets for defining the playing field, roles, responsibilities and outcomes expected in order to achieve individual and group success.

Does this mean that everyone always plays by the rules? Not at all; that is why the operating framework needs to be clearly articulated to everyone. We are all occasional transgressors.

When we step 'off the path,' the principles and skills previously identified provide others with the ability to gently call it to our attention. As in sports, there are also those who are continual and intentional transgressors. When that happens, there are penalties, the option of retraining, and/or the alternative of leaving or being asked to leave the game entirely.

When we step
'off the path,'
the principles and skills
previously identified
provide others
with the ability
to gently
call it to our attention

This chapter outlined some recommended steps that your organization or group can follow to implement this process. These included forming a cross-functional or representative design team to oversee the development, implementation and evaluation.

Obtaining fair representation on the design team and any needed focus groups will help ensure that there is broad buy-in among employees and management

Obtaining fair representation on the design team and any needed focus groups will help ensure that there is broad buy-in among employees and management. Having executives and managers attend the training first ads legitimacy and shows commitment to the process.

The bottom line is that when the conflict mediation process is well designed and implemented, the chances for your achieving identified outcomes are greatly enhanced.

Managing Conflict Every Day

The conflict mediation process presented here provides an effective framework for resolving conflicts at the lowest possible level.

In this chapter, we will describe how to apply this process within the family, friends and communities. You will also learn how the process can be useful even with those who are not familiar with the framework or skills.

Family & Conflict Mediation

Family conflict has been present ever since Adam and Eve argued over who was to blame for eating the apple in the Garden of Eden. Family conflict did not improve very much when you consider their children, Cain and Abel.

As discussed previously, conflict is a natural and inevitable condition that occurs when two or more individuals perceive that their goals, needs or wants are in jeopardy of being frustrated by another. Conflicts within

Family conflict has been present ever since Adam & Eve argued over who was to blame for eating the apple in the Garden of Eden

families can occur due to a wide range of conditions.

Life changes often cause stress that contributes to conflict within families, according to Thomas Holmes and Richard Rahe. Life change is any significant change in a person's personal, family or work situation.

The table in Figure 10 summarizes the top 20 items they identified as major life change events.[8]

Which life events are you experiencing?

_____

_____

_____

_____

_____

_____

_____

_____

Figure 10
Life Change Events

Rank	Life Event	Mean Value
1	Death of spouse	
2	Divorce	100
3	Marital separation	73
4	Jail Term	65
5	Death of close family member	63
6	Personal injury or illness	63
7	Marriage	53
8	Fired at work	50
9	Marital reconciliation	47
10	Retirement	45

Figure 10
Life Change Events (continued)

Rank	Life Event	Mean Value
11	Change in health of a family member	44
12	Pregnancy	40
13	Sex difficulties	39
14	Addition of a new family member	39
15	Business readjustment	39
16	Change in financial state	38
17	Death of a close friend	37
18	Change in different line of work	36
19	Change in number of arguments with spouse	35
20	Mortgage	31

According to Holmes and Rahe, each event's mean value reflects the event's impact on the individual. The death of a spouse is assumed to be the most traumatic event with a point value of 100. Having a mortgage payment carry's a lower point value of 31.

It is interesting to note that the list contains both negative events, such as being fired at work, and positive events, such as marriage and addition of a new family member. It is also interesting to note that several of these life events may occur at the same time. For example, in the same year someone might have a parent pass away, lose their job, become ill and move to a new place of employment. Collectively, these can cause great stress on the individual.

Conflicts in families do not have to be very traumatic to cause discord and unhappiness. In fact, many if not most conflicts occur over what we might consider to be relatively minor issues. Spouses and children often develop conflicts due to misunderstandings, unvoiced assumptions or disagreements over roles or responsibilities. Conflicts may also occur between one individual who means well, but is perceived by another as being inconsiderate. Consider the following case.

Steven is in the living room watching a movie and ironing one of his wife's dress as she returns from a trip to the supermarket.

"Hi Lisa," he says, "Were you able to find everything okay?"

"Yeah just about," she replies as she goes through the living room. "I couldn't find that pasta sauce we really like and..." she pauses as she sees the dress he is ironing.

"You didn't wash that dress did you?" she asks as she puts down a bag of groceries.

Her husband beams, "I sure did. I washed the whole load of laundry and I thought I'd iron a few of your items because I know how much you hate ironing."

Lisa seethes, "I can't believe you were so stupid as to wash and iron a silk dress! Don't you even read the labels?"

"But it was in the laundry basket and..," Steven begins.

"You just ruined my favorite dress. I can't believe you did something so brainless. Why don't you stick to what you do best and just watch TV!" she says as she storms off to their bedroom and slams the door.

Steven wads the dress up and throws it in the corner. "For crying out loud," he thinks, "See if I ever help out around the house again!"

Some of you can probably identify with this scenario. Others may be thinking, "Are you kidding? I'd be glad if my spouse just washed a load of laundry or ironed their clothes once in a while." Poor laundering skills did not show up on the major life event scale that Holmes and Rahe developed, but it is often the 'little' life events that cause so much discord among family members. Family members have disagreements about home chores, allowances, who gets to use the car, what is for dinner, whose

In the space below, describe how you might approach this example differently.

_____

_____

_____

_____

_____

_____

_____

turn it is to clean the litter box, how long one person has been on the phone and what time the kids need to be home from a date.

Regardless of the source, the mediation process suggested in this book can be used to help diffuse and resolve these never ending points of contention. In the scenario above, Steve meant well, but ruined one of Lisa's favorite dresses. Lisa has responded very negatively by attacking Steven personally. Suppose Lisa has been trained in these mediation skills at work?

Let's revisit the scenario and observe how this situation might be handled between someone who understands the process and someone who does not.

Steven is in the living room watching a movie and ironing one of his wife's dresses as she returns from a trip to the supermarket.

"Hi Lisa," he says, "Were you able to find everything okay?"

"Yeah just about," she replies as she goes through the living room. "I couldn't find that pasta sauce we really like and..." she pauses as she sees the dress he is ironing.

"You didn't wash that dress did you?" she asks as she puts down a bag of groceries.

Her husband beams, "I sure did. I washed the whole load of laundry and now I am ironing a few of your items because I know how much you hate ironing."

Lisa sighs, "Steven, I appreciate that you are trying to do something nice. Did you know that the dress you washed and are ironing is made from silk?"

"No, is that important?" Steven responds.

"Yes, silk needs to be dry cleaned. Washing it has probably caused it to shrink and lose its shape. I doubt I can wear it again and that was one of my favorite dresses," she replies. "This is the second time you've ruined one of my outfits and I think we need to talk so it does not happen again."

"Well, I was just trying to be nice. You're the one who put the dress in the laundry basket so how was I to know it couldn't be washed?" Steven replies.

"Look Steven, I don't want to fight over this," she says, "I appreciate what you tried to do but I also want to figure out how to keep this from happening again."

"Okay," Steven says, "So what do you suggest?"

Lisa thinks for a moment and then says, "I think it's safe to say we both want our clothes cleaned correctly. Is that right?"

"Sure," Steven says.

"So if you do the laundry, can't you read the labels and see which ones are not machine-washable?" Lisa offers.

"Look, these all look the same to me. After all, I do sort them by whites and solids already," he counters. "Why not put them in different piles; those that need to be washed and those that need to be dry cleaned?"

"Yeah, I could get another clothes basket and we put the regular laundry in one and the clothes to be dry-cleaned in the other," she suggests.

"I think that will work," Steven replies sheepishly. "I suppose I can tell the difference between a basket full of regular laundry and dry-cleaning."

"That's fine," Lisa says, "But could you also try to read the label if you are even a little in doubt?"

"Yes," he says, "I'll do my best."

"Well you finish ironing and put up the groceries while I go back to the store and get a second clothes basket right now!" Lisa laughs.

If Lisa and Steven had mapped the conflict using the CGA matrix, it would probably look like the information in Figure 11 below:.

Figure 11

Problem: Steven ruined an expensive silk dress because of inappropriate care.

Person	Concerns	Vision	Actions
Steven	• Positive relationship with Lisa • Do something nice for her •	• Help with household chores • Surprise his wife • Do something while watching the game	• Care for clothes appropriately • Place clothes in appropriate basket • Read labels if in doubt
Lisa	• Positive relationship with Steven • Hates having her clothes ruined	• Help with household chores • Provide proper care for clothing	• Care for clothes appropriately • Buy a second clothes basket • Place clothes in appropriate basket

In this scenario, Lisa and Steven are able to mediate the conflict to an agreeable solution. Lisa took the lead in identifying the problem, expressed her concerns and desired outcomes. Note that Lisa relied on her communication skills in following the CGA process. She let Steven know that she did not want anymore clothes ruined, explored alternatives and agreed on some actions they both can take.

The ability to communicate effectively and mediate conflicts within a family is very important. Recall the first scenario in which both Lisa and Steven become angry and the result is unproductive conflict. Consider how much more unproductive the conflict would have been had children been present. Children learn to model the behavior of their parents. If parents are able to model effective communication and problem solving skills, children also learn and employ those skills.

Mediation and Friends

Conflicts don't just happen at work and within the family, they also happen between friends or neighbors. Relationships between friends and neighbors are very important. Friends are individuals we can share our thoughts, concerns and desires. They are often people we can count on to provide advice and support. Similarly, neighbors are the people who live nearby. As with our friends, we socialize with them, let our chil-

The ability
to communicate
effectively and mediate
conflicts within a family
is very important

dren play with their children, visit each others homes and depend on each other for occasional supplies or tools. It is sad and unpleasant when two friends or neighbors have petty conflicts that escalate unnecessarily. Consider the following scenario.

Bob and Carol have lived across the street from Jim and Mary since they moved to the neighborhood three years ago. Bob and Carol have one child, a girl who is six. Jim and Mary have two children, ages seven and nine. The neighbors get along very well, although Bob has noticed that Jim seems much more interested in work and golf than his children. One morning Carol and Mary have gone shopping and Bob is getting ready to go jogging with his daughter. Bob and his daughter like these times because he can push her in a baby jogger through the park and they often stop to feed the ducks. As he is lacing up his shoes there is a knock on the door. When Bob goes to the door, his neighbors' two children are standing there.

"Good morning," Bob says. "What are you two doing today?"

The oldest says, "Dad is going golfing and he asked us to come over here until mom gets back."

Bob looks up at the sound of a car engine and sees Jim beginning to back out of his driveway. "Hey Jim," Bob yells as he walks over to the car. "What's going on?"

"Well, I saw you were home and figured you could watch the kids while I go golfing," says Jim.

"I really can't right now, Jim," explains Bob. *"I'm going jogging with my daughter and can't watch your kids."*

"Come on, you can wait until the girls get back from shopping," snorts Jim. *"Besides, the kids love playing over at your house."*

Bob is beginning to get a bit angry. *"Jim, I'm sorry but I can't watch your kids now. When I get back from jogging, I'll be glad to watch them, but not now."*

Jim glares at Bob and says, *"Okay fine! You go jogging and I'll just wait here. But hurry because I don't want to wait too long to get out on the course!"*

Your initial reaction is probably that Jim is behaving rather thoughtlessly. Unfortunately, that is often how conflicts begin. Like many minor events, this one could become a seed of discontent and mistrust that serves to poison a positive relationship between neighbors.

Care should be taken because the relationship is more than that between Bob and Jim. The relationships also include their wives and children.

Below in Figure 12 is a CGA Worksheet that you can use to map out this dilemma for both Jim and Bob. Let's consider the various aspects of this scenario and see how it might be handled more effectively.

Figure 12
Bob and Jim CGA Wotksheet

Person	Concerns	Goals	Actions
Bob			
Jim			

Compare what you identified with the following. Jim's position is that he wants Bob to baby sit the kids. Bob's position is that he wants to go jogging with his daughter.

What might be their concerns? Jim is concerned with getting to the golf course and Bob is concerned with spending some quality time with his daughter and avoiding being imposed upon.

What might be their respective goals for a positive outcome? For Jim, it might be that Bob stay home and watch the children while he goes golfing, maintaining a good relationship with Bob and giving his children some time to play with Bob's daughter. Bob would also like to maintain a good relationship with Jim, but go jogging with his daughter.

What actions might be considered? Jim could put off golfing until later in the day, some other day or take his children with him to the golf course (they might really enjoy riding around on the golf cart). Bob could put off running until Jim or the wives return, not go jogging at all or just go jogging with his daughter. Can you think of any other options?

The desired outcome of this episode is to avoid having a little thought-lessness blow up into a major event and destroy a friendship. At different times in our lives we are all a bit thoughtless.

By focusing on the facts, at least Jim and Bob can reach some resolution to the conflict. If Bob is able to communicate his position and concerns effectively, he may help Jim see that his assumption that Bob would just watch the children is thoughtless.

Conflict Mediation and Community Groups

We are all members of a variety of organizations. **Occasionally, differences in opinions, action plans and priorities lead to conflicts which can cause one of these organizations to self-destruct, despite the fact that these organizations have beneficial missions.**

It is unfortunate when political agendas, false impressions, micromanagement or misunderstandings cause these groups to become dysfunctional. When these members within these groups become dysfunctional, the damage, stress and unpleasantness erode the effective use of resources, funds, time and energy.

The Group Conflict Mediation Process is very useful for helping these groups discuss and mediate their conflicts so they get back on track.

It is unfortunate
when political agendas,
false impressions,
micromanagement
or misunderstandings
cause groups
to become dysfunctional

[8]Organizational Behavior: Managing People & Organizations. G. Moorhead & R. Griffin, 1992, Houghton Mifflin Company, MA.

Notes

Summary

Organizations, families and community groups need not suffer Organizations, families, and community groups need not suffer as much as they do from the effects of unproductive conflict.

The conflict mediation process recommended in this book provides an effective framework for assisting organizations, work teams, and all kinds of groups to resolve conflicts at the lowest possible level.

This approach reduces stress among those involved, and improves organizational and individual effectiveness and overall performance.

When a group lacks the ability to consistently mediate its own conflict, morale suffers, turnover and absenteeism soars, customer service is eroded and productivity nosedives.

In this book, we have suggested that working groups are not significantly different from professional athletes. Athletes bring well-honed skills and knowledge, coupled with an understanding of the game process and a commitment to engage productively with the team. For this talent and commitment, they are handsomely paid.

Organizations, families
and community groups
need not suffer
as much as they do
from the effects
of unproductive conflict

Executives, managers, employees and volunteers in nonprofit organizations also bring their knowledge and skills to their workplace. Couple these with the skills to mediate their own conflicts, principles for guiding behavior and appropriate incentives to ensure commitment, and they will work toward conflict mediation and a safe environment.

Conflict is an inevitable part of our lives. BUT conflict does not have to mean an all-out war, long term discord or harsh feelings.

Kathy Domenici (1996)[9] observed that in mediating conflict the "parties are not in a contest. The goal is not to find out who is right, who is to blame or to whom to give credit. The goal is to find the appropriate resolution to the conflict; one that satisfies both parties."[2]

Provided the right skills, a shared process for resolving conflicts and the appropriate level of commitment, the level of unproductive conflict in your life, your team and your organization can be diminished.

Conflict
is an inevitable part
of our lives. BUT
conflict does not have
to mean an all-out war,
long term discord
or harsh feelings.

---

[9] Mediation: Empowerment in Conflict Management. Kathy Domenici, (1996) Waveland Press, Inc., Illinois.

About the Author

Garry **McDaniel, Ed.D.** is president of PowerWorks Consulting, firm specializing in working with for-profit, non-profit and government entities to improve organization performance and productivity. Garry brings over 25 years experience developing leadership talent on a global basis.

His background includes establishing high performance mentoring programs, succession plans, strategic planning, organization development, career planning, leadership and management success factors, web-based management tools, performance management, teambuilding and 360 feedback systems. Dr. Mc Daniel is a frequent keynote speaker throughout the United States and Australia.

Contact
Garry McDaniel
at
PowerWorks Consulting
11506 Charred Oak Drive
Austin, Texas, 78759
garrymcdaniel@aol.com
or by calling
(512) 799-4090.

About the Collaborating Editor

Barry Silverberg, First World Library's Managing Editor for Nonprofit Leadership, Management and Organizational Development series,, served as senior editor for this volume. Mr. Silverberg is founding Director of the Center for Community-Based & Nonprofit Organizations at Austin Community College. His 30 years of diverse volunteer and professional leadership wiothin the nonprofit sector includes service as Chief Professional Officer of Jewish Federations in Syracuse, NY and Austin, TX, president of the Texas Association of Nonprofit Organizations (TANO), founder and president of the Syracuse Area Interreligious Council and leadership roles in many other nonprofits.

Mr. Silverberg and Dr. McDaniel are collaborating on a number of othr volumes in the areas of Credible Leadership. and Effective Committee and Meeting Management. He can be contacted at barry@1stworldlibrary.com.

About 1st World Library

1st World Library is in the business of making dreams come true. We enable authors just like you to easily and rapidly transform their works into printed books available for sale to the public. **1st World Library is a self-publishing company.**

If you are writing to share stories, personal experiences, the lessons you have learned along the way, we will help you create a book that will be cherished and shared by others.

If you are writing to facilitate the learning of others, the skills and knowledge that you have gained, we will help you create a book that will become a standard.

If you are writing for posterity, from a sense of responsibility to those that follow, we will help you create a book that your children's children will cherish.

Through our combined experience, the contributions of our partners, and the technology that is available today, we provide you with the best tools

Where your goals are our goals... your dreams are our dreams...

and experience available to self-publish. As an author, you will be supported, encouraged and guided along the way.

Authors interested in exploring self-publishing opportunities through 1st World Library should contact: info@1stworldlibrary.com. Please provide us with a short synopsis of your book (maximum of one page) and your contact information, including the best time for us to call.

Authors' Note: We have found an initial discussion of our services and what you can expect from us is very helpful in making your decision. During this initial discussion we will explain the self-publishing process clearly; you will then understand your responsibilities and just how much you can expect to spend.

Brad Fregger
Founder/President/CEO
1st World Library - The World's Publisher
brad@1stworldlibrary.com
(512) 339-4000
www.1stworldl.ibrary.com

Index

O

Operating values 109
Opportunity Costs 13
Organizational values 35

P

Physiological needs 39
Pilot 115
Position 47, 48
Power management 35, 36, 43, 111
Principles 10, 15, 17, 29, 35, 108, 109
Process 10, 15, 17, 29
Process facilitator 44
Process leaders 44
Process Leadership 35, 36, 43, 112
Process mediator 90
Productivity Costs 13
Professional athletes 17

R

Rahe, Richard 122
Reframe 76, 78, 79
reframe 78
Respond 42, 80, 81, 82
Responding 79
Restate 76, 77
Roll-Out Plan 115

S

Safe environment 35, 36, 39, 110
Safety and security needs 39
Self actualization 39
Skills 10, 15, 18, 29
Sources of conflict 22
Systems 16

T

Team 30
Team Leaders 113
The Magic of Conflict 14
The Seven Habits of Highly Effective People 49
Third Party Mediation 85, 86, 87
Training 113

U

Unproductive conflict 5, 9, 13, 16, 21, 27, 137

V

Values 36, 38

Notes